The Pe

A '70s Memoir

Jim Landwehr

ELECTIO PUBLISHING
first century principles.
a twenty-first century approach.

The Portland House: A '70s Memoir

By Jim Landwehr

Copyright 2018 by Jim Landwehr. All rights reserved.

Cover Design by eLectio Publishing

ISBN-13: 978-1-63213-466-0

Published by eLectio Publishing, LLC

Little Elm, Texas

http://www.eLectioPublishing.com

*Portions of this book have been previously published in *Neutrons/Protons* magazine, *Steam Ticket*, and *Zest Literary Journal*.

5 4 3 2 1 eLP 22 21 20 19 18

Printed in the United States of America.

The eLectio Publishing creative team is comprised of: Kaitlyn Campbell, Emily Certain, Lori Draft, Court Dudek, Jim Eccles, Sheldon James, and Christine LePorte.

Publisher's Note

The publisher does not have any control over and does not assume any responsibility for author or third-party websites or their content.

This book is dedicated to my mother,
Mary Lou,
whose unceasing love, patience, and kindness
made our sometimes crazy house a home.

Acknowledgments

I would like to recognize a few people who helped make this book possible. First and foremost, my mother and my siblings. They are the story before you. Their influence, personalities, and support over the years helped shape me into the person I am today, and I am grateful for their ongoing presence in my life. Along those lines, I have to add that the accounts herein are as I remember them and I've written them primarily in the name of entertainment. In so doing, I in no way intended to vilify, demean, or defame any of my siblings. They are family, I love them, and they made our life on Portland beautiful.

I would also like to thank Michael and Kathie Giorgio and all of my colleagues at AllWriters' Workplace and Workshop, particularly the Mighty Monday Nighters. Their critiques and encouragement spurred me on whenever the evil inner critic took a foothold. Endless thanks and prayers of gratefulness and glory go to God for His protection and provision for our family during those formative years on Portland Avenue. As crazy as it may seem, I also owe a bit of credit to the band Pink Floyd, whose music powered me through the writing of this book. And, finally, none of these words would be possible without the support from my wife, Donna. She recognizes my passion for the craft and is my biggest cheerleader. I love her more than anything.

Contents

Introduction

A HOUSE IS NOTHING MORE than a carefully assembled collection of bricks and mortar, wood and nails, windows and doors. It's when you blend it with the stew of six kids, a recently widowed working mother, and any number of stray pets that things get interesting. When this happens, there is always a runny nose, a leaky faucet, an emotional breakdown, a small fire, a wall in need of paint, a limping pet, a sparking appliance, or a small pool of blood. I refer to this collection of energy as life. Growing up, life is what happens inside the walls of our homes every day. It shapes our character, bonds us together as family, and ultimately forms our past that comes out whenever we say, "When I was a kid ..." And while my circumstances were slightly different from most for the time period—a large, single-parent family in the '70s and early '80s—the experiences we had, the struggles we endured, and the obstacles we overcame are common to families of all sizes and all time periods, I suspect. Everyone had a family, we all grew up in homes, and while life wasn't always *Leave It to Beaver*, it made us who we are, and that is mostly beautiful.

A bit of background is necessary to set the stage for understanding what made this house on Portland Avenue in St. Paul, Minnesota, so special for our family.

There were seven kids in our family, all born within a ten-year period from 1955 to 1964. From oldest to youngest it was Tom, Pat,

1

Linda, Jane, me, Rob, and Paul. Linda passed away tragically in March of 1961 at the age of five after battling a Wilms tumor. Mom was pregnant with me at the time and between pregnancy, the pull of the other three children, and keeping a household, she barely had time to mourn the devastating loss of our sister. Dad changed jobs frequently and money came and went. As a result, we lived in a couple of houses on short-term rental arrangements. These were hard times for our young family.

At this time in the mid-'60s, my mother and father were going through some marital struggles as well. Dad had difficulty working through the grief of losing his daughter and never really recovered from his mourning. To add to the mix, he was a restless soul, never completely happy with his various jobs. He worked construction for a while and then pharmaceutical sales. Over the years, his grief, discontent with his work, and the strain of trying to be a father to six children took its toll and he started drinking. His vice became a bad habit and escalated to the point where he and Mom were arguing a lot. Eventually, they separated and, when she was still pregnant with Paul, the youngest, we moved into her father's house on River Road for a spell. It was extremely cramped and Mom wanted to get out as soon as possible. Broke with six kids, she was forced to apply for government housing, and we moved to the McDonough housing projects in East Saint Paul.

While the six of us were living in the projects, my father was living alone in an apartment on Selby Avenue. On June 28, 1967, he was brutally murdered in a hate crime assault by a gang of African-Americans at Happy Harry's bar in the Selby-Dale neighborhood. Details remain sketchy to me, but from what I understand, he was picked out of the crowd at random and beaten. When the gang was cleared from the bar, my dad was helped to a chair and said, "I didn't deserve that." These were some of his last words. The gang returned and beat him a second time, including a blow to the head with a crutch, fracturing his skull and killing him. It was a racially tense time in our country's history and he was an innocent in the wrong place at the wrong time. This does not in any way absolve him of the fact that he had a family of six kids to care for and he shouldn't have been there. But *no one* deserves getting beaten to death. Ever.

Sometime after Dad's death, Mom found a small house for rent on Hubbard Avenue about two miles from the Portland house. It was a considerable step up from life in the housing projects, but the house was small, cramped, and, among other things, had a bug problem. To add to the mix, we had a nosy, meddlesome neighbor who had issues with Mom. The next door neighbor didn't like the fact that Mom had come dragging six kids along with her. All the while, Mom knew the Hubbard house was a pause, not a stop, in our journey. She began thinking about moving shortly after we'd moved in and we ended up living on Hubbard only about a year. As a seven-year-old, I inadvertently did my part to incite a move by starting a raging good closet fire while playing with matches. Luckily, Tom and Pat came to the rescue and put out the blaze before the whole house went up in flames.

The Hubbard house really served as a springboard to greater things. It gave Mom a taste of independence from having neighbors stacked up around us like shipping pallets. More importantly, it gave her a freedom from the stigma of living in the projects. Thank goodness low-income housing was available for tough times like we experienced, but Mom's pride wouldn't allow her to live there any longer than necessary. She felt we needed a place to set down roots, a house of her own to raise us, preferably within a good school system.

Mom came upon the house on Portland during her trips taking Rob and Paul to the babysitter. It was just down the block from where she dropped them off and she took note of the for sale sign. After passing it a few times she decided to take a look inside. During the showing, she loved it so much she immediately started to work toward making an offer. She was doubtful a widow with six kids would ever qualify for a home loan, but she applied anyway. To her surprise, she got the loan and once she was approved, the owners accepted her offer. In December of 1969, with the help of Tom, Pat, and Mom's friend Joyce, she moved our belongings from Hubbard to Portland, and we began our new lives in our new house.

And finally, it is worth noting that, while Mom single-parented the bulk of our years at the Portland residence, she had help from her boyfriend, Jack, whom she dated for nine years before marrying in 1979. Jack was a divorced man with eight kids of his own. His kids lived with their mother, whose name was, ironically, Mary. Even more ironically, their house was only two blocks away on Portland Avenue. So, at one time there were two Mary McKasys living on Portland. I know. Weird.

This book aims to take you back to this place with all of its inherent chaos and love, its stopped-up drains, burnt toast, and beeping smoke alarms. But because our house was part of a neighborhood and because neighborhoods, in turn, make up a city, we will wheel down the block, stop in the local schools and shops, and make our way around the city a bit. St. Paul holds a special place in my heart. It is the younger, smaller, snot-nosed brother to Minneapolis. It has a downtown with big city feel, yet not so big you ever get lost. But, if you do manage to get lost, just go to the Mississippi River, take a left, and you'll be back downtown in no time. After I moved to Wisconsin in the mid-'80s, at holiday time people frequently asked, "Are you headed back to Minneapolis for the holiday?" To which I replied, "Yeah, heading back to Saint Paul." I made the intentional correction because it mattered—to me at least. So, I would be remiss if I tried to write about the house I grew up in without including the surrounding context which made it so special in the first place.

So open up a bottle of pop, preferably Tab, if you have it, put a hot dish or a chicken pot pie in the oven, settle into that bean bag chair, and come back to the '70s with our big family. It's okay, you can spend the night. I'm sure it's fine with Mom.

Chapter 1 - Porch

THE HOUSE WAS SQUAT AND STRONG. It sat on its foundation with a sense of heaviness and permanence. It was built in 1907 when houses were made to last, not just fill a lot on a subdivision plat. Architecturally, the house had great balance. The front porch featured four Romanesque pillars that held up its roof. The smooth round pillars were painted forest green, like the rest of the house, and stood sentinel with their darker green curlicue ornamental caps. They sat on custom-made concrete bases that created the transition from the heaviness of the porch foundation to a sense of lightness and lift at the roofline. The pillar bases were painted the same dark green that matched the rock foundation. The floor of the porch sat three feet off the ground and was solid concrete for its length. Like the rest of the house, it was put there with the intention that it would stay there for a hundred years or more.

Hot summer afternoons were spent on the porch by me, my five siblings, and any of our gang of friends. It was a haven on a rainy day where we could stay dry and still be outdoors. For a period of time, a porch swing hung from the ceiling. One day, one of the long screws that held it into the tongue-in-groove wooden ceiling finally gave up its hold. Along with its seated audience, one end of the swing came crashing to the porch floor. I'm not saying that perhaps it had been overloaded with too many kids, but I'm not denying it either. Nonetheless, it was another of Mom's home improvement attempts that fell victim to the destructive forces of a large family of kids.

The raised open porch had a bit of a challenging allure to it from a kid's standpoint. When I was eleven, I bet my younger, more naive brother, Rob, a quarter he wouldn't be brave enough to jump his bike off the three-foot-high drop to the lawn below. At this time in the early '70s, Evel Knievel was all the rage and every kid wanted to be able to jump his bike over or off something significant. Rob was no different. He was hesitant at my first offer, but after he haggled me up to fifty cents, it became a challenge he couldn't refuse.

He sized up the jump a couple of times. Starting at one end of the porch, he measured the length in pedal rotations on his Schwinn Stingray knock-off. Then, he backed up and measured again. This exercise was as much for courage building as it was an estimation of mechanics and distance. To make the jump and actually land on both tires would require building up a fair amount of speed, likely unachievable given the short twenty-five-foot runway he had to work with. Logistically, it was like trying to launch a Boeing 747 off the deck of an aircraft carrier. The physics of the whole maneuver just didn't add up. This leap to fame was doomed from the start. To make the jump even more precarious, bicycle helmets were still years away from being mainstream and, if they had been, it's likely we wouldn't have worn them anyway. Back then, we were left to use our own skills and faculties to traverse the many dangers of day-to-day living. Things like car seats were poorly designed and only used as an afterthought. Lord knows I never sat in one. Most of my car time was spent bouncing free in the back seat with only other siblings to act as human airbags in the event of some disastrous crash.

Nope. Rob was forced to take his daredevil jump with no safety gear other than his Wrangler jeans, a dirty T-shirt, and a pair of blue bumper sneakers. He took a deep breath, gave me one last look, and started pedaling toward the end of the porch. He barely got two rotations of his pedals cranked when he hit the lift-off point. His attempts to pull the front end of the bike up to ensure a parallel landing with the ground were in vain. His front wheel plunged nose-first off the edge and Rob quickly became a member of the over-the-handlebar club when the back end cartwheeled behind him. He landed on his shoulders and somersaulted forward onto his back. The bike crashed down in an inglorious heap at the base of the porch, right next to where the chalk outline would be drawn of my poor brother, whom I had certainly just killed in the name of personal profit.

Oh my God, what had I done? I'd likely just paralyzed my brother for a lousy half a buck!

I rushed down the steps and around the porch and was elated to find him picking himself up and brushing himself off. He staggered around dazed, checking himself for missing or broken appendages. He was bleeding from his lip and appeared to have the wind knocked out of him, but to his credit, he was up and walking like a prizefighter after a seven count.

He's alive! Dear God in heaven, he's okay, I thought. My stay in the penitentiary for manslaughter was not guaranteed after all. Rob walked unsteadily past me and said, "You owe me fifty cents. I'm gonna go lay down." The whole event was, at a minimum, a paralytic near-miss, but it was also indicative of the kinds of recklessness that life before video games and cell phones brought to kids. We did these things in the name of entertainment. It was part of the price of being told to "go outside and play."

We were just doing what we were told.

***

FROM THE STREET, there were two sets of steps that took you to the porch. The first set was a seven-step climb to get up the hill from the front public sidewalk. It was necessitated by a steep grassy hill that traversed about a five-foot change in elevation. It was the hill Mom affectionately referred to as a "bear to mow." There were two methods to cut the grass on this slope. The first entailed starting at the bottom and mowing parallel to the hill's grade with a zigzag cut. The higher up the hill the mower got, the sketchier the whole process became, as the mower threatened to roll over if one wasn't careful. The second technique involved long-arming the machine down from the top to the middle of the decline, then strong-arming it from the bottom up to the middle. I credit being quick on my feet with not cutting one off during one of the many rolls back down the incline. Overall, I'd have to say Mom's assessment of the hill was pretty much spot on.

The second set was five steps bookended by thick concrete railings. These steps and railings formed an outdoor think tank for making important kid decisions like whether to play a pickup game of baseball or walk down to the drugstore for candy and a little small-business loitering. The steps also served as the perfect venue for a game we called step baseball. The game was played between two players, where a tennis ball was thrown against the steps by the batting team while the fielding team stood on the other end of the ricochet and tried to catch the ball before it hit the ground. Skill came into play as you tried to guess whether the batting team was going to throw it softly in hopes of it dropping short for a base hit or haul off and send it airborne all the way down to the hill steps. Reaching those stairs constituted a home run, unless the fielder wanted to blindly navigate them and rob the batter of his glory. And, true to the sport, there were also foul balls that deflected up onto the porch and banged the glass panes of the lantern-style light hanging from the porch ceiling. Over time, a couple of these panes were shattered by errant tennis ball fouls. Needless to say, Mom wasn't quite the same fan of the game as us boys were.

Two windows that looked into the living area were spaced out along the porch's span. As you approached the house, on the left was an extruded three-sided bay and on the right was a huge picture window with a separate leaded cut-glass portion adorning the top. This decorative glass was used elsewhere on a few ground-floor windows and created brilliant refractions that exploded into the living room when the sun hit them. It was a nice touch of class to an otherwise utilitarian home. The picture window beneath these decorative panes served as our glimpse into the outside world, our Gladys Kravitz porthole to the neighborhood. I recall many days sitting on the couch with the drapes drawn, watching a good old-fashioned Minnesota snowstorm building to a roil.

Above the porch roof were three windows, one for each bedroom, boys on the left and girls on the right, and a third smaller one for the closet centered between them. This construction lent a pleasant balance to the second floor. Regarding the smaller window, I always thought it strange a closet would need a window. Frankly, I never spent much more than five seconds in any closet and if I did, it certainly wasn't to check the weather. But evidently there's an architect out there who either grew plants in the closet or had a problem with small windowless spaces.

The fact that the two bedroom windows opened onto the porch roof served to help us kids use them as a chance to get an elevated perspective of the neighborhood. It was a great view from up there. Mom always hated it when we ventured onto the roof, but that did not stop us. In fact, it was my sisters Jane's and Pat's favorite place to lay out and get a tan. For us boys, it served more as a launching place for toy parachutes, water balloons, or the occasional bottle rocket. It's certain our neighbors loved us.

The exterior of the house was wrapped in two-inch wood siding. As a result, every six years or so, it needed a coat of paint. Because of the heavy traffic near the front door, this siding took a beating. Eventually a board came loose and over the summer, a cluster of yellow jackets found a gap and made their home under the backside of the newly exposed siding. My brothers and I noticed that there was a regular comin' and goin' of bees to and from a narrow entry point. For a while, we feared and avoided the pests for worry of being stung. Summer has a way of boring kids into acts of stupidity, however, so the hive was not to go undisturbed for long. We took the pest control task into our own hands one day when our neighbor Matt from across the street brought his Wiffle bat over looking for something to hit. On top of suffering from late-summer brain paralysis, Matt was pretty fearless. He saw the bees' nest as a source of amusement. It was like a 3D adventure movie for him.

He grabbed the plastic bat and approached the hive's entry point with caution. To his credit, he was careful to time the incoming and outgoing flights before he began his folly. When there was a three-second gap between arriving and departing bees, he wound up and whacked the siding three times at the entrance.

That served to agitate the bees just a bit.

It was a siren call for the bee colony. Everyone out! The bees started climbing and stumbling out of the entrance with speed and regularity. At least we had the good sense to vacate the area. We scattered and ran serpentine to minimize the casualties. Every once in a while, one would zero in on one of us and motivate us to kick our running up a notch. It was an every-kid-for-himself mentality. This was our bee war.

After a few minutes, the bees returned to their roost and their frenetic demeanor slowed to its normal pace. Wanting a part of the action, I reached out to Matt.

"Hey, let me have a whack at it," I said.

"Here you go. You gotta be quick, though," Matt said, as though he was the bee whisperer or something.

I courageously stepped up to wreak my havoc. Like Matt, I timed the arrivals and departures like an insect air traffic controller. Intending to outdo him, I took four quick whacks at the hole. By the fourth swing, things were getting busy at the exit, my cue to quit. I dropped the bat and took off like a base runner with the game on the line. After getting in the clear in the front yard, I watched the nest activity until it resumed its normal pattern again. It took a little longer than the first time as the bees were starting to ratchet up their "nasty" a bit.

The bee tormenting continued until someone was either stung, or we lost interest. It was the simplest form of pleasure available for boys looking to kill some time and maybe a few pesky insects while they were at it. I guess today's kid might be more likely to spend that time pushing a game controller or a joystick or thumbing a smartphone. Our joystick on this day was the Wiffle bat and, much like the video games of today, you never knew what you were going to get from play to play. I'm sure some would beg to differ, but it seems that ours was so much more real, so much more fun.

Chapter 2 - Living Room

THE FRONT DOOR OPENED into a small entryway and a coat closet with a vinyl accordion door. This entryway was closed off by a heavy door with a plate glass window that opened to the living room. The closet was a catch-all for coats, shoes, boots, and gloves. On at least one occasion when Mom wasn't around, it served as a truth-or-dare kissing booth for one of my sister Jane's middle school parties. Because everyone knows there's nothing like being enveloped in coats and boots in a dark confined space to jack up the romance.

Directly ahead of the entry was the stairway to the second floor. To the right of the stairs was the spacious and welcoming living room. The floors were covered by hunter green carpeting, one of the favored colors of the early '70s. On the far wall was a fireplace that drew the eye's attention immediately upon entering the room. Constructed of painted white brick with a marble apron, it served as the central showpiece of the living room, if not the entire house. On either side of its upper mantel shelf rested a pair of brass lamps with hurricane globes. These lamps were never plugged in for lack of nearby electrical outlets, but gave the fireplace a homey character nonetheless. Below, on the middle mantel shelf, Mom displayed an arrangement of artificial flowers.

The irony of this beautifully constructed fireplace was that it was entirely non-operational. Built in 1907, it, like many fireplaces of the time, was built as a coal-burning unit where the coal was burned in baskets, intended to give off a little extra heat. We discovered this the hard way on the couple of occasions we tried to start a blaze in it. I remember my stepfather igniting newspaper and logs in an attempt to get a fire going. As he stacked the logs, he remarked that they seemed to be too close to the fireplace apron to be safe, that the fireplace wasn't deep enough. Once it was ignited, his observation came to life as it seemed the fire was just a little too close to actually being *in* our living room. The lack of depth meant that the chimney inadequately drew the smoke up, as well. Within minutes, the living room was smokier than a Marlboro-sponsored monster truck rally. After standing back amongst the fog building at the ceiling and surmising for a moment, Jack surrendered and put the smoky fire out. In later years, one more attempt was made to disprove the "coal only" label placed on the fireplace, but it failed much like the first.

Despite its functional failures, it still served a purpose as an ornamental fireplace in front of which nearly every significant family snapshot was taken. Events like graduations, proms, and weddings. One of the more iconic photos was snapped at Christmas in the early '80s, when we were all young and healthy. The boys were standing tall in the back, Mom and sisters in front, Jane a few months pregnant in a maternity dress. Everyone was smiling and looking happy. The little-known reason we were all smiling was because Tom was standing on his tiptoes at the time, trying not to look the shortest of all the brothers.

The picture evokes the sum total of what made up our family. Siblings wearing everything from maternity dress, to college sweatshirt, to a coat and tie; equal parts family, fun, and success. We are gathered in the living room we grew up in, smiling at the antics of the eldest and trying to look regal for a photo. Front and center stands Mom, the catalyst behind all the beauty and success and promise that surrounds her. She is both the foundation and the mortar that held us together. The picture exudes happiness and love. It was our finest hour.

***

THE LIVING ROOM WAS ALWAYS respectably furnished considering our brood. There was a pair of couches, one in front of the picture window and the other aligned next to the dining room entrance. These couches took a beating at the hands of us kids. It seemed one or the other was always in distress, slated for replacement at the next tax return. Usually the fabric began to fray and separate from the frame at the stress points. This was when the bed sheet "cushion covers" came out, surely every interior designer's nightmare. Even the most color-coordinated living room loses something when two-year-old sheets become the upholstery du jour.

We had a light brown floral sofa that eventually fell into the secondary couch category. Because of the constant abuse, one back leg broke off. It was broken either during a couch wrestling match between two siblings, or because it was dragged instead of lifted while rearranging a room. My guess is the former. Mom fixed the leg for the short term by using a large can of Dinty Moore Beef Stew in its place. After a period of time, the other back leg broke and all it took to fix it was more stew. It actually made the couch more balanced because there was no height difference between the two legs. This jury-rig approach seems so low class looking back, but let me tell you, when you're living it, it makes perfect sense. Mom was on a limited income and she was doing her best to keep the household up. As a homeowner today, it's no different now around my own home. You fix what you can afford, and what you can't gets propped up on stew cans or strung together with duct tape and Gorilla Glue.

***

OUR LIVING ROOM HAD TWO cast iron radiators in it, both painted white to match the walls. The boiler in the basement sent hot water to and fro, providing a nice, moist hydronic heat throughout the house. Every fall, Mom sent one of us around with a radiator key and a bowl to "bleed" the air out, making the radiators more efficient for the coming winter season. The long radiator near the bay window was always a popular spot to sit and warm up on those January mornings. You came away with a good case of ripple butt, but it sure took the edge off before heading into your morning routine.

In the corner closest to the dining room sat our television. The first couple of years it was a black-and-white with big aerials and a UHF ring antenna. These were the days when the channel options were a grand total of four and, on a good day, maybe five or six if you were able to seine a decent signal out of the UHF band. Eventually we upgraded to our first color 19" model from Sears. I remember watching *The Wizard of Oz* in color for the first time. It was nothing short of dazzling. The color televisions of the day were antiquated compared to the models of today. Most of them had a dizzying array of tubes and capacitors and weighed as much as an anvil. Ours always had aluminum foil crimped onto the aerials in an effort to magically clarify the picture. It seemed to help. It made one wonder why manufacturers didn't just make them that way in the first place. Anyway, when the tinfoil trick wasn't working, the old standby of slapping the set on the side usually took care of things. TVs were funny like that. And if it didn't fix the picture, well, at least it felt good.

As our set aged, its picture degraded. Part of this was just aging technology and part was user-driven by the constant adjusting of the contrast, color, and tint dials on the front, to say nothing of the side-slapping. We pushed and fiddled with these dials until the picture was visibly over-contrasted or colorized. Then we reversed the process and backed it down until there were minimal shadows and the actors on screen returned to shades approaching the human skin tone spectrum. Because everyone around the house had a different definition of "optimum" color and clarity, the set never had a chance. It was in a perpetual state of adjustment and readjustment.

Above the television, a wandering Jew plant hung from the ceiling in a macramé plant holder. Mom had a knack for unintentionally killing these wandering Jews with great consistency. This caused her to confess some Catholic guilt and remorse when the subject of her gardening skills came up. There's something shameful about the thought of killing any Jews, even if it was only a plant. I once made the mistake of watering one of these plants without taking it down from its holder, only to have the excess water run out the bottom of the pot and into the back of the TV. After realizing my error, I quickly took the plant down and switched on the set. The colors and picture were skewed and scrambled. *Oh my gosh, I've killed it!* I was mortified. The TV cost hundreds of dollars! Fortunately, after a few hours or so, it eventually dried out and returned to normal. It's a wonder the whole set didn't short circuit and melt down. I'm not sure I ever confessed my deed, but I was certainly relieved when the picture came back.

***

ONE SUMMER DAY, as I sat on the couch in the living room, I heard a loud crack on the window behind me. I quickly craned my neck, only to see a hole about the size of a half-dollar in the glass. A web of cracks radiated out from the hole in the lower corner and a small rock lay on the interior sill. I looked out to see my brother Rob and a friend standing in the street and Rob holding his Wrist Rocket slingshot in his hand. It appeared they were trying to gauge where their shot landed. I flapped my arms wildly, shouting, "Oooooohhhhh, you're in trouble! Look at what you did. You busted the window! I see you!" I shouted to no one but myself as there was no way they could possibly hear me through the glass. Never mind the fact that Rob was deaf and wore hearing aids. I stood there, cackling and doing my accusatory chicken dance for a few seconds to make sure he saw me, before I went out the front door to confront him and his friend. I walked across the lawn and down the hill to where they were. Sensing his shot had gone afield from its target, Rob tried to make the slingshot a little less prominent, holding it behind his back.

"Did you see what you did? You busted the picture window!"

"I didn't do that."

"I see your slingshot and it just happened, so if you didn't do it, who did?" I countered.

"Oh, please, please don't tell Mom. It was an accident," Rob begged.

Mom found out, of course. I don't recall if I ratted on him or if he made a full confession and threw himself at her mercy. As with most situations where we were kids being kids, she was upset, she was angry, but she was merciful. I always admired this quality in Mom. She did her fair share of brow furrowing and finger shaking, but in the end, she didn't lose her temper too often. As a single parent trying to raise six of us, her demeanor was firm, but laced with loving respect, and she expected the same from us. When we were disrespecting each other, she let us know it and she didn't tolerate it. We were family, doggone it! When we did wrong, she let us know it but then she moved on and never put into doubt her love for us. Her love overrode any material possessions and she never held grudges, that much was clear. When you're running a household of six, forgiveness needs to be applied liberally.

My older brother Tom removed the broken glass later that day. It was summer and it was just a storm window, so the interior one would serve until a replacement could be paid for and installed at a later date. Unfortunately, that date came sooner than expected. A few weeks later, the interior window was broken by a BB gun shot from the neighbor kid across the street. Luckily we witnessed it happening and mom followed up and saw that justice was served in getting the parents of the offender to pay for it. It was a rash of bad luck for our big window, just another series of aggravations for my poor mother who was just trying to keep the pets in and the elements out.

The living room picture window was our fish-eye lens to the outside world. From the comfort of the living room, we watched the world go by. We saw traffic on Lexington Avenue, observed what the neighbors were doing in their yard half a block away, and gauged what the weather held in store. Having the window shattered twice in the span of a month provided a peek into Mom's character as well. When Rob broke it with the slingshot, she could have lost her temper and made a huge deal out of it. She chose to take the high road, and, while the incident upset her, she used it more as a teachable moment than a chance to humiliate. With the neighbor, she kept things peaceable, but was bold enough to confront the perpetrator and see to it that justice prevailed. The big window was part of her castle. Most of the time, the castle was all she had going for her in her effort to raise us. When the windows of the fortress were broken, it called for correction and justice and Mom carried it out with authority, tenderness, and finesse.

***

IT WAS NEW YEAR'S EVE in 1973 and Mom was at a downtown hotel with Jack, whom she was dating at the time. My younger brothers and I were sitting at the top of the stairs eavesdropping on my sister Pat's high school party rollicking down in the living room. The three of us were in our pajamas and were relegated to our room when things got started at about eight o'clock.

"You boys stay in your room and don't come out. I'm going to have some friends over," Pat said.

We were never informed that it would be half the varsity football team.

The cigarette smoke and noise drifted up the stairwell to our room. Teenagers were laughing and talking ridiculously loud as Led Zeppelin blasted from the cheap department store stereo. Because we couldn't resist a little harmless spying, a quick peek revealed that most of them were drinking Schmidt beer from "Big Mouth" bottles, a popular bottle-style marketing trick of the mid-'70s. The laughing and joking was nearly constant, with the deep baritone voices of the men-boys supplementing the higher-pitched shrill voices and laughter of the girls. I wasn't sure what could make everything so screamingly funny, but was pretty sure cigarettes and beer played a big part.

The situation was both alluring and alarming to my twelve-year-old mind. I worried that my sister would get in trouble for hosting such a blowout. The legal drinking age at the time was eighteen and many of the kids were probably of age, but many likely were not. I was more worried than the rest because I was the family goody-

goody and I specialized in worry and rule-following. This was in addition to a chronic condition of self-righteousness, judgment, and piety. On-premise drinking and smoking will raise the anxiety level of any goody-goody.

Every so often, there was a thump that shook the floor as the football players brought their game into the living room with some roughhousing. Between that, the wailing of Robert Plant, and the squeals of Pat's girlfriends, the house was rocking. Mom's bed was piled high with coats, proof that the living room was undoubtedly packed beyond its capacity.

At the same time, there was an attraction to the madness going on downstairs. Like moths drawn to the flame, my brothers and I could not seem to stay in our room and ignore the chaos. We peeked through the spindles of the banister like nasty little voyeurs. The thought that my sister was doing something inherently wrong, which could get her into deep trouble, had a certain sinister appeal to it. This party went against everything I knew to be right and good, yet they sure sounded like they were having fun. For us boys, being confined to our bedroom meant we weren't, so we snooped from the top of the stairway.

Eventually, Pat was tipped off that we were spying on the goings-on and started up the steps toward us. The three of us fled to our room and shut the door. She barged in and began her lecture.

"I told you boys to stay in your room!"

"We saw your friends smoking cigarettes and drinking beer!" I said.

"Well, very observant, Sherlock. And you better not tell Mom, either."

"I'm going to," I threatened.

"C'mon, Jimmy, please? All my friends are here and we're having fun. What's wrong with that?"

The case-pleading and idle threats went back and forth like this for five minutes until I eventually relented and swore not to tell

Mom. Pat returned to the chaos downstairs and Rob, Paul, and I closed our bedroom door and regrouped. Like prisoners in our bedroom cell, we did what any little criminals would do; we plotted blackmail. For Christmas that year, one of our gifts was a black, top-loading cassette deck, the kind used for interviews and simple recording. Paul came up with the idea that it would be fun to tape record the conversations downstairs so we would have some incriminating evidence. If nothing else, it would be fun to listen to the craziness and see what was being said.

Paul plugged the microphone into the unit and popped in a cassette tape. We cautiously opened the bedroom door and scanned the hallway. With the coast clear, we crept out to the top of the stairs. Paul clicked on the recorder and held the machine while Rob fed the small black microphone between the spindles of the staircase. It dangled there suspiciously against the white walls near the ceiling of the living room. Had we given it any thought, we might have spent a little more time in disguising the mic. It was clear that espionage was not our forte. Nonetheless, we were poised for our own little Watergate bugging. This was our Partygate.

After a few minutes, we heard one of the football players say, "Hey, what's that thing? Patty, I think someone is recording us!"

We told Rob that we'd been ratted out and he quickly pulled up the surveillance device, as we scrambled to get back to the safety of our bedroom. We slammed the door and heard the telltale thumping on the stairs. Pat, wanting us to know she was ticked off, used a little extra lead in her step. Clunk, clunk, clunk, up the steps she came.

The door swung open wildly and she shrieked, "What's going on in here? Somebody said you were recording us. Where is that tape recorder?"

Rob pulled it out from underneath the bed and handed over the deck to Pat. She took it, saying, "All right, all of you, listen up. You need to stop spying on us and stay in your room! And I don't want you coming out or I'll make your lives a living hell."

She was well into what I'd call a good start.

***

BY THE TIME I REACHED COLLEGE, I began following in the footsteps of my siblings by throwing occasional house parties of my own. The planning of these affairs began immediately upon hearing that Mom was leaving town with Jack for a getaway vacation. To her, I was the well-behaved one, so she didn't expect it from me. These parties were a sort of rebellion, I guess. A way of acting outside of the kid I was perceived to be. And because I wanted my parties to have their own unique flair, I gave them a theme. At the time, I was a huge fan of George Thorogood and the Destroyers, a raucous rock and roll band. My friends all knew of my fanaticism, so when I decided my theme was to be "A Tribute to George Thorogood," they were not surprised. In the weeks leading up to the date, I prepared invitations and mailed them out.

> *Come one, come all to the House of Blue Lights as we pay tribute to George Thorogood and the Destroyers.*

People were amused when they got the invitation to my first George party. The affairs soon became an annual tradition and, after the second or third consecutive year, I'm fairly certain my friends thought I had a screw loose. I used the House of Blue Lights tagline because George did a cover of that song and most of my friends knew of the song. I even went so far as to string a strand of blue Christmas lights on the front porch around the bay window. They served as a beacon for the partygoers and gave the house a festive quality. They probably functioned as a guiding light to the cops and nosy neighbors as well, but that was a small price to pay for the novelty of the idea.

In 1983, when I was twenty-two, my mom and stepdad gave a couple of weeks' advance notice that they were headed out of town for a weekend getaway. I immediately drew up the invitations, made copies, and mailed them out to twenty of my closest friends. Two weeks later when Mom and Jack pulled away from our house on Friday afternoon, I set to work. The first order of business was to hang the blue lights. I sprinted up the attic stairs and pulled a few strings of lights out of the holiday decoration box. These were the big bulbs that used to be commonplace on all Christmas trees—the kind that burned nice holes in your carpet if you let them dangle low by accident. I quickly switched out all the colors in one of the strings to blue and headed back downstairs. I hung them around the bay window and rigged them so they could be plugged into an extension cord in the living room.

Next I went to work setting up the stereo. This required moving the whole system from my bedroom to the living room. Just as I was bringing down one of my large floor standing speakers, I saw my stepfather's car pull up in front of our house.

What the . . . ? No, this can't be happening. They're supposed to be gone!

I panicked and set the speaker down as far out of sight as possible as they walked up the front steps. I met Mom at the door. "Hi, Mom, what are you doing home?" I asked, trying to stifle a grin of guilt.

"Well, we decided to stay in town tonight and just go tomorrow."

I stood there shocked, just blinking.

"Oh, and uh, why are there blue lights on the window?" she asked with a convicting smile.

"Lights? What lights?" I said, grinning.

I knew I was busted and she knew their surprise visit after a short drive worked out perfectly. Mom and Jack chose to take the high road on this little exposé. They had a laugh and went out of town as planned. I breathed a sigh of relief and finished setting up for the big bash. In the tradition of years prior, I played each of Thorogood's albums in their entirety. Much like my sister's affairs, it was a rowdy good time with lots of music, beer, and laughter. A spontaneous, albeit brief, dance party even broke out in the dining room for a song or two. Like most of my parties, it was a police-free event. Always a bonus.

The next morning the kitchen smelled like a frat house basement and the keg bobbed in the tub of melted ice. The house of blue lights had become the house of the morning after. My head throbbed as I started my dutiful cleaning. Over the years, Mom knew of my parties, but we had an agreement of sorts. Provided the cops weren't called during them, and the house was cleaned afterward, she didn't much care what went on, within reason. And if there was one thing I made very sure of, it was to clean the house meticulously after these blowouts. It set the ground for next year's party and gave her a clean house to come home to. It was a win-win scenario and we both kind of knew it.

***

CHRISTMAS AROUND OUR HOUSE was a time of great anticipation, excitement, and buildup. Mom always tried to make the holiday perfect and memorable for all of us and, to her credit, always seemed to pull it together. Sometimes it was at the last minute, but it was always done with beauty and warmth. She was masterful at the details, like hard ribbon candy in decorative dishes around the living room, lots of candles, and a big bowl of unshelled nuts with a nutcracker on the end table. Decorative garland was wound around the spindles of the stairway and our stockings, which she'd made herself when we were young, were hung with care by the dysfunctional fireplace. Mom knew what Christmas meant to kids, and having six of them meant going the extra mile.

She made her annual phone call to Santa from the kitchen on a Saturday a few weeks before Christmas and we were explicitly banned from the room during the exchange. For someone worried about long distance charges, this one to the North Pole never seemed to be a concern. And, evidently, Santa used the Montgomery Ward Christmas catalog as a reference for his gift requests. At times, we overheard Mom rattling off SKU numbers to the elven clerks on the other end. It struck us as odd that Santa would need a reference number from a catalog, but as long as he didn't backorder the all-important gifts we wanted, his methods of manufacture and distribution were insignificant.

A week later, after picking up the order from the Ward's catalog dock, Mom took large garbage bags filled with gifts and stashed them away in the attic for wrapping at a later date. When she found time, she wrapped them and put them back up in the attic until the big day. One year, when I was about eleven years old, I sneaked up to the attic to size up my take of the haul. I used the age-old technique of pressing the gift wrapping tightly against the box for a couple of my larger gifts and was able to read the labels. I discovered one of the packages was a race car set I'd asked for and another was a Clue game. I felt a strange mix of joy and shame at my findings—joy at the thought of getting what I really wanted and guilt for having breached the trust of my mother, who was trying to ensure our hopes and expectations were met on Christmas Eve. When Christmas finally came, it was highly anticlimactic. I swore to myself I'd never cheat the system again.

***

CHRISTMAS EVE WAS ALWAYS loud and brash and full of laughter and joy at the house on Portland Avenue. On one particular Christmas Eve, in 1983, the relatives started arriving about five o'clock. Along with my brother Paul, I was a student at the University of Minnesota. My brother Rob was home from Rochester, New York, where he was attending college. My older siblings, Tom, Pat, and Jane, were all moved out and raising families of their own. They arrived on this night with kids and spouses in tow for the annual gathering at Mom's. Everyone was in high spirits, exhausted from all the preparation, yet finally ready to let down and enjoy the night with family.

After the welcoming hellos and Merry Christmases were said, people began settling in. Beers were opened among me and my three brothers while the ladies opted for wine. Sisters Jane and Pat chose to live dangerously, sipping "the recipe," a concoction named after moonshine peddled by the two sisters on *The Waltons* television show. My sisters' was a tempered version featuring Bailey's Irish Cream as a base, but still packed a punch. Mom flitted between the living room and kitchen, worried about whether the standing rib roast was done or not. Our grandmother, Dagny, sat in the overstuffed chair, looking regal in her Christmas outfit and costume jewelry necklace, sipping a cocktail of her own and laughing her Barney Rubble laugh that I loved so much. Every year, all of us dreaded the slobbery goodbye kiss from Dag, whose lips were always unnaturally wet at kiss time. The ritual had become an annual joke between us, one we looked forward to in a twisted sort of way. It wouldn't have been Christmas without it.

Dinner's main course was the traditional roast beef, accompanied by green beans, mashed potatoes, gravy, Dagny's oyster casserole, and a crystal bowl full of my sister Pat's mysteriously good "Green Stuff." The dish acquired its quirky name a few years prior when someone asked, "What's this green stuff?" No one quite knew what it was called, so the name just kind of stuck. It seemed an appropriate name for the merriful mix of pistachio pudding, whipped cream, and fruit cocktail. The dish was great despite everything that is wrong with the idea of combining pudding with a fruit mix.

After the food was set out, a line formed at the antique buffet, which was filled with platters and bowls of steaming, fragrant food. One by one the adults filled their plates and took their seats around the antique dining room table set with Mom's fine china and sterling silver cutlery. Delicate crystal goblet stemware held wine or water. Tapered candles burned in the middle of the table, warming the room as it buzzed with laughter, stories, and compliments on the meal. The food smelled savory and delicious. It smelled of love and richness and Christmas.

The children were relegated to the kids table in the kitchen with a paper tablecloth, plastic cups, and paper plates. A teenager or two sat with them to oversee the carnage, conduct damage control, and keep them focused. The kids picked fussily at the little servings of food chosen by hopeful parents. Most of them were full from too many cookies and candy treats, the rest simply too wound up and excited to eat.

When dinner was finished, an annual tradition had the Landwehr/Kaufenberg/McKasy men clearing the table and doing the dishes. Sisters Jane and Pat joked about how nice it was to see the boys working for a change, and even nicer how good it was to see them all working together. The discussion over dishes jumped from world issues to what was wrong with the Vikings' running game. The mood was jovial and anticipatory, each of us men stifling our expectant happiness at opening our gifts, which happened when the last fork was dried. The love of Christmas has no age limit.

With Tom being the eldest sibling, Mom declared it his year to pass out gifts, a job once handled by our grandfather or an uncle. Tom settled into the designated Santa chair near the ornately dressed Norway pine and started reading the names. "To Mom from Jane. To Paul from Dagny," and so on as he worked through the pile. Nieces and nephews served as helper elves and ran the presents to each of the recipients. Carols seeped from the stereo and a light haze of cigarette smoke began to form near the ceiling from the smokers in the group. Two Un-Candles, a trendy '70s sensation that burned vegetable oil as fuel, sat on the mantel, warming the room with their glow. The moment was frenetic with half a dozen conversations going on during the present distribution. The young kids were shrouded in electric energy, barely able to suppress their pent-up excitement. Through all of it, God swirled about the room whispering in each ear.

"Do you see this? Isn't this beautiful? Revel in it. Hold it. This is Me. This is love. This is My love."

When the last gift was distributed we dug in. There was no taking turns among this group. Each person tore and unwrapped at their own pace. The kids ripped with voracity while those with fewer gifts took time to watch and enjoy others' moment of happiness. The room buzzed with a medley of cacophony and chaos. Shouts of "Thank you, Mom!" or "Oh, I love it!" echoed across the room with regularity and gratitude. Gasps were plentiful and dramatic. People spontaneously tried on the sweaters, slippers, and hats they received. Toys were unwrapped as parents chimed warnings to the children.

"Watch those small pieces! Every year something gets lost or thrown away in the wrappings. Hey, save the bows."

It was a momentary, unbridled free-for-all of excess, greed, and gratefulness, and I loved every minute of it. As the gift opening neared the end, my brothers and I all secretly held out one last present, trying to be the last one to open something. It, too, was one of those meaningless traditions that took on a life of its own one year and continued on into perpetuity.

Everyone reveled in their gifts for an hour or so before they started packing things up for the ride home. As midnight approached, Rob and I prepared to go to Midnight Mass across the street at St. Luke's. The two of us went every year and it became something I looked forward to as an escape from the noise and confusion as well as a reminder of why we gather in the first place.

We walked across the parkway, down the streetlight-lit night, and filed into the cavernous church, dimly lit for arguably the biggest service of the year. We genuflected and took our place in a pew near the middle. We kneeled and prayed quick prayers of thankfulness and settled back in our seats. The huge pipe organ fired up the first notes of "O Come All Ye Faithful" as the congregation stood for the processional. The lofty music rose and fell and, combined with the harmonies of the choir, lifted my spirit skyward. Later in the Mass, the priest lit incense and shook the metal thurible back and forth in each direction, filling the church with aromatic, smoky, floral joy. The whole experience was powerful and reminded me of the true meaning of Christmas.

After the long but beautiful service, Rob and I headed out into the cold darkness for the walk home. Our frozen breath hung in the air as we talked about the neighbor girls from up the block that we saw in church, and how they'd become beautiful young women now.

Then, when I least expected it, Rob hockey-checked me into a snowbank, where I landed hands-in-pockets, in a heap.

He ran away laughing and shouted, "Merry Christmas, bro," while I was left to dust myself off and take chase through the frozen night in my dress shoes. In a full sprint, I was shocked, damp, and laughing as I slipped and slid down the street. I was equal parts amused at my brother's trickery and annoyed at my own naiveté. I should have expected it from him. Time transcended—it was a moment of sibling goofiness carried into adulthood. There we were, grown men being boys on Christmas Eve.

We arrived home winded and still laughing at Rob's practical joke. We cracked one last beer and settled in the living room for a bit of wind-down, a few more Christmas carols, and one last gift assessment. The house was quiet and the air still hung with the smell of food, smoke, and candles. When we finished our drinks, we unplugged the tree lights and headed up to our bedrooms.

It was, in every sense of the word, an average Christmas. There was much preparation going in, and the inevitable letdown after the last gift was opened. At the same time, it was a small moment of perfection, a glimpse of heaven, or maybe a peek into the fiery heart of God's eternal love. My brother Rob passed away in 2011, and as a family, we're over thirty years removed from this Christmas night on Portland Avenue of so long ago. Despite his absence, my siblings and our mother continue to pass down these traditions to our own kids and to his. Christmas Eve is a night filled with the love of family surrounded by food, merriment, gifts, hugs, and warmth. We've taken to attending service at the Methodist church in Minneapolis with Rob's wife and daughters when we can, and the words and hymns mean as much as they did at St. Luke's so long ago. And while the players have changed, the principles of family, love, and togetherness remain steadfast. Yes, perhaps these average Christmases are all we can expect and hope for from year to year. My thought is that if they satisfy the souls and spirits of my children like they did for me, well, that is plenty enough.

Chapter 3 - Kitchen

OUR KITCHEN WAS AVERAGE-SIZED and equipped with shiny, harvest-gold-enameled appliances. The refrigerator was a trendy side-by-side model with sorely inadequate freezer space, a quality my mother always griped about. Her grumbling script was rerun every week on shopping day. Mom's weekly Tuesday night trips to Red Owl grocery a few blocks away brought home six or seven paper grocery bags of food, and four gallons of milk. After unloading the groceries from the car, the task of stuffing the frozen products into the tight, narrow spaces of the freezer commenced. It was equal part art and science, a bit like the handheld sliding puzzle games we played as kids. Slide the hamburger left, frozen pizza up, tater tots down, ice cream right, and slam the door fast. It was a Rubik's freezer. This unlovable refrigerator came with the house when Mom bought it, so we sort of put up with it until it finally died. Mom replaced it with an over-under model that had considerably more freezer space in the top section. On shopping days, packing it was still a puzzle game, but at least it had an easier solution.

We never had a secondary chest freezer in the basement like some families and it's unlikely the electrical infrastructure of our house could have handled it if we did. Fuses blew regularly, usually the result of someone running a hair dryer at the same time the Kirby vacuum was being used. To deal with it, boxes of every available amperage sat like spare rolls of toilet paper on top of the fuse panel in the basement. If one blew, the offending party was required to go down and shine a flashlight in the box and look for the fuse with the charred out window. We'd find a matching color and wattage amongst the spares and plug in a new one. It was a Band-Aid on the gangrene wound, but fixed the problem for the moment. Mom's philosophy was, fuses were cheap. Rewiring the entire place was not.

Next to the refrigerator sat the color-matched electric stove. This was an appliance placement strategy I never fully understood. It was probably because there was no other place for it in the kitchen, but to put a device that heats next to a device that cools seemed bass-ackwards to me. I picture the architect getting the plans all done just in time to present to the owner, only to have his boss point out the poor layout. In any case, because of the way the walls and counters were cut, there was really no other workable configuration, so we lived with it.

The exterior walls of our kitchen were poorly insulated. During heavy winter winds, you could practically fly a kite in the kitchen breeze. Furthermore, it was situated on the northwest corner of the house, an area that rarely got sun and always caught the brunt of the arctic-cold Canadian air. The whole room was heated by a single, laughably small radiator. The pitiful thing looked to be more an afterthought than an adequate heat source for even the mildest of Minnesota winters. It meant that on bitingly cold winter mornings when temperatures were below zero, Mom broke down, turned the oven to preheat, and opened the door. She was brutally aware that it was an incredibly inefficient and expensive way to heat the kitchen, but frankly, she didn't care. It was a third-world solution to our first-world problem, but a person has their limits. Sometimes, it took two or three kids complaining about it to get her to cave in; other times, she just did it of her own volition. It was her house, and by God, she was going to be comfortable, whatever the cost. Sometimes, it's good to be queen.

Next to the stove, on the side opposite of the refrigerator, white, confetti-patterned Formica countertops made a ninety-degree turn and ran the length of the west-facing wall. The counter was divided in the middle by a stainless steel double sink. Below it and to the right sat our built-in dishwasher. In our big household, this poor appliance took a serious beating. For starters, it was run with great frequency because of the never-ending stream of stipple-textured green drinking glasses, stoneware plates, and Tupperware bowls. Our poor loading techniques also stressed the washer in a number of warranty-voiding ways. Popcorn seeds were sucked through the rotating spray arm, clogging the jets. On multiple occasions, Tupperware lids fell through to the heating element and were melted into disuse. But perhaps the most destructive practice involved using the open dishwasher door as a step to reach an item in the cupboard above. All of us younger kids were guilty of this expensive stepstool. Repeated strain on the door eventually bent the hinges, which in turn created a bad seal between the door and the frame. The rest of the story involves a wet floor, a new dishwasher, and a stern lecture from Mom on what the door was really for.

Our abuse of the washer meant that it was frequently out of service for long stretches. During these downtimes, we were tasked with washing the dishes by hand, a job we all hated. Disdain for this chore led to us taking turns doing the dishes from week to week. A week of dishes sounded like an eternity as a kid, but we knew once it was done, we were free for a period before it was our turn again. Regardless of whose week it was, heaven help the person who did not have them done by the time Mom got home from work. There were times when we put the dishes into the sink to soak while we went out to play. This inevitably meant they were left forgotten until Mom got home. When she found the dishes soaking in tepid, suds-less water, well, suffice it to say the lioness roared. These kinds of incidents drove her crazy, rightfully so. Getting dinner ready after a long day at work was hard enough without one of us washing the breakfast dishes at the same time.

One day in my middle school years, when it was my turn to wash them, I went to the sink to fill it and when I turned on the water, it flowed out of the faucet blood red. *What the heck?* I quickly shut it off in disbelief, thinking it was a temporary thing. I turned it back on and got more blood water. I was befuddled. What was going on? A massive fish kill in the water supply? Was our house possessed? A Biblical plague perhaps?

I tried the water a third time to see if it would run itself clean. The red water continued to flow. I moved the knob to the hot position with no visible change. *Whatever it is, it's in the hot water too!* I quickly began to get creeped out.

"Hey, Tom, the water's all red," I yelled.

Tom walked in from the living room. "Really? Show me."

I turned it on and the toxic water flowed again. Tom said, "What? Wow, that *is* weird. What does hot do?" I switched it to hot and showed him the same result. "Hot too? Huh." After a few seconds of pondering, he couldn't contain himself any longer and burst out in laughter. "I can't do this. This is too easy," he confessed.

He unscrewed the screen filter on the faucet and pulled out a red tablet. It was one of those plaque disclosure tablets that they used to give students to chew after brushing their teeth, to see how well they were brushing. After chewing, the tablets turn areas of plaque dark red and the rest of your mouth a light pink. Tom brought some home from school and thought it would be a good joke to play on one of us. As the oldest sibling, it was Tom's job to educate us on the ways of the world. Sometimes this took the form of a practical joke in order to teach us that life is not always what it seems, that our innocence sometimes makes a sucker of us—especially me, the biggest sucker of them all.

When we were done, the two of us put the tablet back in the screen for the next sucker.

***

ONCE A WEEK OR SO, Mom tasked one of us kids to get dinner in the oven so it would be ready by the time she got home from work. One of the more common meals involved one of us putting pork chops in a pan after school at 3:00 and spooning a can of mushroom soup over the top. Then we put it on "Timed Bake" to start at 4:30. We thought nothing of it at the time. When I told my wife of the practice years later, she was a bit horrified we left meat in the oven at room temperature for that long. Looking back, it would have probably made an interesting biology experiment in bacterial mutation. I can't say for sure that, over the years, a few of these sorts of meals weren't put in the oven in the morning before she went to work, which is scarier still. Luckily, we all lived to tell about it and, frankly, the pork chops were delicious.

A staple side dish with many of our meals was baked potatoes. Those actually worked quite well in a timed bake scenario. Mom directed us to wash six spuds, cut the ends off, and poke some holes in them so they wouldn't explode. The first time my wife made baked potatoes, she poked holes in them and that was it. I told her she needed to cut the ends off. She looked at me as if I was speaking Swahili. "Why would I do that?" she said.

"Well, Mom always told us to cut the ends off," I answered defensively.

"Why would you cut the ends off? Think about it. If you poked holes in them, why would you need to cut the ends off?"

"Uh, I dunno. I was only doing what I was told."

I had to admit, she had a good point. The next time we were home visiting my mom, I had the chance to ask her. "Mom, you know when you used to make us cut the ends off potatoes when we'd get them ready for the oven? Why did we do that?"

She looked at me quizzically and said, "Uh, I don't know, actually. I always did it because that's the way my mom did it."

So, there you have it. Absurdity transcending the generations.

Along with potatoes, another staple at our house was hotdish, the unofficial Minnesota state food. In other states and regions, people call it bakedish or casserole, but we all know those are incorrect nouns. Put it in a dish, serve it hot. Hotdish! It is a Minnesotan's way of snubbing the work involved in preparing multiple courses. It's easier to just throw them all together in one pan and call it dinner. I think its popularity with the large families of the day was because it was easy to prepare, could be served in the dish it was made in, and required only a side of bread. It meant easy prep, easy cleanup, and no tending during the baking process. It was our comfort food and we loved it.

Mom had a handful of these recipes at her disposal. There was a chow mein hotdish, which had the noodles baked right in it until they were soft and then topped off with crunchy ones after it came out of the oven. Another family favorite was mozza' pie, which was a deep dish pizza-type entree featuring a hamburger crust. Tuna casserole, beef stroganoff, and spaghetti pie were all hotdish offshoots that were hits with the family. There were countless other varieties including chicken wild rice, scalloped potatoes and ham, and the dreaded green bean mushroom soup compilation. Sometimes they took on their own kooky localized names like hamburger noodle pleaser or chopped meat noodle dish. At our house, my personal favorite was a nameless macaroni recipe made with hamburger, tomato paste, onions, and green peppers. It was usually served with "homemade" bread that, while it was baked at home, was really just frozen store-bought dough. In a pinch, Hamburger Helper could be substituted for a meal of hotdish, but it was never as good as the real thing.

These culinary amalgamations were a Minnesota staple in the '70s and the recipes and traditions behind them live on throughout the upper Midwest. They enabled families to gather around the table and get their fill of meat, vegetables, and starches all in a single meal. There is no doubt that some recipes are the butt of jokes—every potluck gathering and every family has a story about one, it seems. The one that has that secret ingredient that should have stayed secret, or the one that people take a tablespoon of just to oblige Aunt Rose and not appear rude. Of course, not everybody was a fan of the all-in-one dish and it is probably snubbed by the upper class as a middle-class meal prep give-up. But for our family, at least, hotdish on the table meant no one left hungry. There was always enough for everyone. The portion that didn't get eaten was easily reheated as leftovers. All of this made Mom's job just a little easier and our home just a little homier.

***

THE KITCHEN ON PORTLAND had one oddly unique characteristic. The floors were covered in a low-cut harvest-gold carpeting. I am certain the designer who made this decision was either single, childless, or some sort of interior decorating deviant. What compelling reason can anyone come up with to justify carpet in a kitchen? After all, what do most people fear about their carpeted rooms? Spills. Where do the most spills in the house occur? The kitchen. Great, let's carpet it.

Mom took the initiative right from the start and covered almost the entire floor with long, clear vinyl runners, the kind with the sharp carpet grippers on the bottom. The runners were highly effective in keeping the dropped jelly and spilled milk stains off of the floor, but they gave the kitchen an industrial look. They also soiled quickly, so every few months, she made one of us roll them up, take them into the backyard, and scrub them. The mats were heavy and bulky for us kids, but with the promise of a dollar or two, we took on the chore. When we lifted them off, we always marveled at how clean the carpet was when compared to those sections that could not be covered. It was actually quite eye-opening as to how dirty the carpet *would* be if we had no runners. It was also proof-positive that there is no good place for carpet in a kitchen. Ever.

In the center of the kitchen sat a table and eight chairs, three on a side and one on each end. It was nothing special; utilitarian and simple. Formica-topped with metal legs, it was expandable and had a couple of those small gaps between the leaves where crumbs and mysterious gunk gathered. The chairs were avocado green with high squiggly ornamental backs made of plastic. Like most homes, each person had their assigned seat and it was honored as such during meals. It's interesting to postulate how we chose the seats we chose, and why we ended up in the configuration we did. The seats were never formally assigned; they were simply claimed at that first meal so long ago and never relinquished. I suspect this pre-set seating goes on at most every table in America. We tend to get comfortable and even territorial about our spots.

Though we didn't eat dinner around the table every night, Mom was pretty good about getting us to eat together several times a week. Everybody seemed to have their little food idiosyncrasies. Jane was a piler. She piled the things she didn't like into a corner of her plate and then covered them with her napkin in hopes of not being called on it. I was the picky one, rarely trying new things and tending toward the old standby comfort foods like meatloaf, pot roast, and pounds and pounds of potatoes. My sister Pat always claimed it was why I looked so anemic—all those starches. Meanwhile, Pat was notorious for her "train wrecks," where she opened her mouth and did a chew-and-show when we were least expecting it. It was a tactic Jane thought was so funny that she started doing it. All of us boys were left to call out these gross displays of impropriety or answer with a train wreck of our own. Yes, we were a pretty highbrow bunch.

At mealtimes, you never knew what kind of surprises were going to come up. Once at dinner, Mom was having a hard time keeping a straight face for the whole meal. We kept asking her what was up and she just smiled and said, "Oh, nothing. I'll tell you later. Pass the pork chops." She then winked a quick wink at Rob, who kept quiet and grinned guiltily. It was very peculiar behavior, but we were hungry, so just continued to eat our pork chops, mashed potatoes, and gravy. When we were done, we demanded she tell us what her little secret was. She grinned and said, "Rob spit in the gravy as I was making it," she said. All of us groaned and gagged. It was a secret that we wished she'd kept to herself.

***

IT WAS SUPPOSED TO BE just another average day after school in 1974. Come home, change into my play clothes, do the dishes, watch *Gilligan's Island,* and go out and play. That's how it was supposed to work. I had my chores to do, just like everyone else did back then and dish duty was one of them. Because Mom occasionally had bacon with her poached egg in the morning, there sometimes was a frying pan with a thick coat of white solidified bacon fat awaiting the dish person. We all hated washing dishes, especially the pots and pans, but one coated in pig fat just made it worse.

There were typically two methods of cleaning this pan. There was the "spat and splat" method where we took a spatula and scraped the grease onto it until it was piled nice and high. Then we walked over to the wastebasket and gave it a good whack until the grease splatted against the side of the garbage can liner. This method, while effective, did not produce a pan that was as pristine as the second method, the "melt and pour."

The melt and pour was conducted while the dish person was waiting for the sink to fill up with suds and hot water. We turned on the burner of the harvest-gold electric stove underneath the bacon pan and in a minute or two, the grease melted enough so that the reliquefied fat could be poured into a tin can pulled from the trash. This entailed a precarious exchange between a middle schooler with a hot pad, a heavy pan of hot grease, and a tin can receptacle. It usually came off without a hitch, and when it did, it resulted in a pan that was much easier to clean, which could be accomplished by simply dipping it in the sudsy water and wiping the residual grease away.

On this given day, I chose to use the melt and pour. Dishes were a chore to be dealt with as quickly as possible so I could get on to bigger and better things. I got home from school, went into the kitchen, and clicked the burner under the bacon pan to medium heat. This would melt the grease good and fast and I'd be done with the dishes in no time. I ran upstairs and changed out of my dark blue pants and light blue golf shirt, the standard parochial school uniform of St. Luke's. Like most boys, I hurriedly pulled my pant legs off inside out and let them fall where they may and then did the same with my shirt. Then I raced to put on my jeans and my T-shirt. Then, for no apparent reason, I wandered into my mom's room and started looking at family photo albums. We had a pile of them and I always loved looking through their thick plastic-covered pages. I sprawled out on her bed, opened one, and started paging through. It is fun reliving moments of our lives using pictures from the past.

Look, that's when we were camping at St. Croix State Park with the McKasy family.

Oh, I remember the Christmas I got that football!

Wow, nice beehive hairdo, Mom. Groovy pantsuit too.

I flipped through page after page, and fell into a fantasyland known only as the past. Each page conjured up a different emotion spun from a different memory; the joy of vacation, an old pet, or the warmth of a family group picture.

Look at Pumpkin! So cute. He was such a good dog.

There's a great fish picture.

The albums were a magnet of nostalgic pull. Like Alice in Wonderland, I fell down the rabbit hole and couldn't seem to climb out.

Hmmm, who's cooking something? Holy crap, the bacon pan!!!

I pushed up off the bed, spun around, and dashed out the door. I leapt down the steps three at a time, took a turn at the landing, and leapt down the last four steps on a dead run. I turned from the living room into the kitchen and could hardly believe my eyes. There was a six-inch cloud of white smoke swirling on the ceiling. It was surreal. I had come from a tranquil stroll down memory lane to a scene from *The Towering Inferno* in a matter of seconds. My eyes shifted from the smoke to its source. The pan of grease on the stove was in full blaze. The flames shot a foot high from the pan and the smoke was billowing, dieseling out at an unbelievable rate. How could so little grease create so much smoke?

Holy crap, I am gonna be in so much trouble for this!

I grabbed a hot pad, knowing that the pan's handle would be flaming hot. I turned off the burner, picked up the heavy flaming iron skillet, and put it in the kitchen sink. Rather than spending time looking for the baking soda, I preferred to take the quick, albeit unrecommended method of extinguishing the inferno by turning on the faucet. All I was thinking at that moment was, this fire needed to be put out by any means necessary, so I could begin the disaster cleanup before anyone else got home.

Using the faucet was a very bad idea.

It was a little like trying to put out a campfire using gasoline. When the water hit the greasy pan, there was an explosion of steam and smoke that leapt off the pan with mushroom cloud fury. The fire parted like a flaming red sea where the water hit as greasy smoke curled upward in billow after billow. I coughed and recoiled as the cloud hit me square in the face. I wondered how so much smoke could come from a fire that was in the process of being put out. Wasn't the smoke supposed to stop? The plume just went on and on like a nuclear blast, most of it steam from water hitting a pan that was probably three hundred degrees.

After I ran the water for ten seconds or so, the fire was out and I shut the faucet off. I looked up at the cloud of smoke above my head and began to wonder what life at the orphanage would be like. Or perhaps there was a special place in Hell for boys with a history with fire. It seemed a good fit given all I'd heard of the place. As luck would have it, no one else was home at the time, so I decided a quick cover-up was the best plan. Perhaps a little fast action would prevent anyone noticing a significant kitchen fire took place since they were last home.

These were the irrational thoughts of a seventh-grade mind.

My first order of business was clearing the smoke. I opened the windows over the sink and flung open the back door. I ran to the living room and opened the front door and a couple of windows. Back in the kitchen, I grabbed a towel and started fanning the smoke toward the opened back door in desperation. The large cloud on the ceiling dissipated fairly quickly, but the residual smell of grease cloaked the downstairs like a death pall—like bacon napalm. Yes, sir, there was no escaping it. There had certainly been a fire in this house today and there was no way anyone entering could miss that fact.

The place smelled like a dumpster fire. I could have spent the next six hours trying to cover up my crime and it still would have been patently obvious to anyone with a nose.

My sister Jane was the first to stumble upon the scene of the crime. I met her in the living room and tried to divert her attention. "It smells horrible in here. What happened?" she asked.

"Really, does it smell that bad?" I asked, hoping to downplay the severity of my bacon fat Hindenburg disaster.

"Yes, it really does. What did you do, start a fire?" Jane asked as she sniffed the air with a measurable degree of "I'm glad I'm not you" in her voice.

"Well, yeah, I did. The bacon pan caught fire when I was melting the grease, but it's out now."

We went into the kitchen and assessed the damage. "Oooooh, Mom's not going to like this," she said, as if I needed reminding.

"I know, I know," I pleaded in my defense.

"Oh my gosh, Jimmy, look at the ceiling!" Jane giggled as she stood on a kitchen chair and rubbed her index finger on the kitchen ceiling. It left a finger streak in the greasy coating that covered the surface. She started laughing that knowing laugh kids share when they feel sorry for their offending sibling, who may spend the rest of their lives in foster care. My shoulders slumped when I saw the incriminating finger mark and realized that the ceiling would likely have to be washed, at a minimum, and perhaps even need repainting entirely. My fears were compounded by the fact that Tom just painted the kitchen only a few weeks prior. I feared his wrath even more than my mother's. There was never the threat of physical punishment by anyone in our family. Sometimes, though, the verbal ridicule and tongue-lashing you got from Mom or a sibling were worse than any blows we could have taken. In most cases, these verbal beat-downs were well-deserved and ultimately served as character builders for each of us.

Mom arrived home at the usual time after work, close to five o'clock. When I broke the news to her, she was justifiably upset. I fully expected her to raise her voice, resulting in a miserable evening for, not only me, but the rest of the family as well. Despite my fears, she was surprisingly forgiving in a pitying sort of way. She had a knack for knowing when we were vulnerable and truly sorry and pulled back on the punishment reins a bit. She said it was a stupid move on my part and she hoped I'd learned a lesson. I admitted I had and reiterated my apologies.

Tom was a bit less forgiving. When Mom broke the news to him, Tom exclaimed, "He did what?"

Once he got over the initial shock and anger, he cooled down and assessed what it would take to clean up the ceiling. As it turned out, he was able to scrub the ceiling fairly easily using a sponge mop. To his credit, much like our mother, Tom usually showed compassionate mercy when one of us messed up. For all intents and purposes, he was the man of the house, so felt the need to assert himself during moments where a father's correction or advice would be relevant. When he confronted me, he reminded me how boneheaded what I had done was. But he did it in a tone that was corrective, not demeaning or cruel. In the end, family safety triumphed over the fact that he had to clean up after his younger brother's mistake. Enforcer, advisor, and corrective officer were all parts of the job of being the eldest and he played them pretty well.

Chapter 4 - Boys' Room

WHEN WE FIRST MOVED INTO THE HOUSE, Mom was faced with assigning six kids to three bedrooms. The house had four of them, but if there was one thing for certain, Mom was getting her own bedroom. The divisions for the remaining three were clearly set from the start. Tom, being the oldest as a fourteen-year-old, would get his own and Pat and Jane, being the only girls, would share one of the larger ones at the front of the house. That left Rob, Paul, and me, all of us under ten years old, to the largest bedroom, also in front. Over the years, this bedroom configuration changed a few times as kids moved out, but in those early years we were all a little cramped.

In what was simply referred to as the boys' room, Rob and I shared a queen bed, and Paul got his own twin by one of the windows on the opposite wall. For myself, this sleeping arrangement was an upgrade. At our previous rental residence on Hubbard Avenue, I slept on a trundle bed pulled out from underneath Tom's twin. At the time that seemed like a fun place to sleep, except on occasions where I was used as a step into, or out of, the twin bed above me. In our new digs the spaciousness of our sleeping quarters and the fact that Tom had his own space made all four of us happy.

Underneath our queen bed I stored my NFL electric football game, a mammoth-sized toy that consumed the better part of my middle school waking hours. I asked for it for Christmas in 1973 and wanted it more than anything else on my list. It could have been my only gift and I would have been content. On Christmas Eve that year, after all the presents were distributed, I looked at my pile and there were no gifts possibly big enough to be it. I sat there bewildered, stupefied, and forlorn. Hadn't Santa-Mom gotten the memo? I thought my wish list had been blatantly clear. After all, I had clearly placed multiple asterisks by the football game. He-She must have seen it!

I tried to contain my disappointment and not let it bother me. Then, all eyes turned to me as my brother and sister pulled the huge wrapped box out from its hiding place in the dining room and pushed it across the floor to me. My jaw dropped. There was no mistaking what it was. I tore into it and screamed, "Thank you, Mom! Thank you, thank you, thank you!" It was a Coleco brand and featured the Minnesota Vikings and Green Bay Packers, which made it even better. I was ecstatic, and still look on it as the best Christmas present ever.

On many winter afternoons, my friend Marty and I played the game in the boys' bedroom for hours on end. We knelt next to the field, him on one side, me on the other, and lined up our eleven plastic players, painted in their true team colors, purple and green. When we were finished assembling, I clicked the switch on and the men began slowly vibrating toward one another. The miniature man with the ball crawled slowly toward the line of scrimmage. The linemen ahead of him methodically buzzed forward at a snail's pace, doing their best to spring the ball carrier free—but strictly on their own time. The suspense was gripping! After a minute or two, the runner squeezed through an opening and suddenly hooked arms with another guy from his own team. They began a slow, circular waltz that stagnated the forward progress of the runner. They twirled round and round, neither one able to release the other to freedom. Instead they pirouetted and rumbaed to the hum of the metal gridiron while their teammates shook, rattled, and eventually wandered aimlessly to the sidelines or the opposing end zone. The action was intense!

When we finally concurred that the play was going nowhere, I flicked the kill switch and we began the whole process again. Marty grabbed his players and set them up in painstaking fashion, and I followed suit. The plastic teams were lined up tight when a running play was called and spread out for passes. In both cases, it took a few minutes to get things lined up before I flipped the switch again. Every so often, one of us inadvertently knocked the board with our knee or foot and the men jumped out of position or fell over, which required starting our meticulous lining up procedure all over again. Much like the real sport, ninety-five percent of the game was spent setting up and unpiling. The other five percent was reserved for real action or, in this case, real slow action.

After an hour and a half of this miniature madness, the interest level began to wane. Now when two of the figurines started waltzing, I bumped up the speed a bit in an attempt to amuse us. The metal field began to rattle and the teams started to quake and bounce frenetically. The noise from the game was alarm-clock shocking. We loosened the vibration screw a bit more and the racket became downright deafening. We plugged our ears as players started to fall over and spin spastically in tiny circles, dancing Irish jigs together in unmanly fashion. Before long, every last one succumbed to the shuddering metallic surface and fell over. Marty and I laughed at the devastation, packed the game up, and wandered off to find something else to do.

***

OUTSIDE THE WEST-FACING BEDROOM window of the boys' room was a gutter that fostered monstrously thick icicles in winter, partly due to the poorly insulated attic. In the boredom of our Christmas breaks, these icy pillars glistened and taunted our middle school minds from behind the closed windows. Unable to resist the temptation, we saw harvesting them as a challenge to be undertaken. Our method to capture them involved using a ski pole and carefully threading the basket end of the pole through the bottom of the icicle. The expectation was that it would break free from the gutter and the fat end of the icicle would catch in the basket. This would allow us to bring the frosty stalactite back through the open window in a feat of deft icicle wrasslin'.

Looking back, there were so many things wrong with this operation that it's almost hard to fathom. For starters, there was the wide open window in the middle of winter. Then, there is the question of what we would do with a four-foot icicle in the bedroom if we were successful in hauling it in. I don't recall that ever actually happening anyways, as shocking as that may seem. More often, we inadvertently knocked the icy spear off the gutter and sent it to its shattering end on the sidewalk below. I have no doubt the neighbors were taken aback by this peculiar, albeit benign exercise being conducted outside our upstairs bedroom. I am also fairly certain these same neighbors must have assumed we were raised on a diet of lead paint chips with a side dish of stupid. Surely nothing short of something this severe could cause such erratic inexplicable behavior from the children within.

But mostly, we were bored and just having fun.

***

IT WAS THE MIDDLE OF THE NIGHT when I was awakened with the crushing need to go to the bathroom. My eleven-year-old bladder was full and in need of relief. Rob was asleep next to me in the big queen bed, and Paul was across the room snoozing in his twin. I got up quietly and went to the door. When I got there, I saw a string tied to the knob. I look closer in the darkness to find it was booby-trapped with a pull-string ladyfinger firecracker. Earlier in the week, my brother Tom acquired a bunch of fireworks, including these ladyfinger devices. The explosives had strings coming out of both ends and were intended to be tied to a handle and a jamb. They were deployed by pulling both strings, so when the door was opened, they would ignite and go off with a bang. It was a harmless explosion, but one that would surely wake my brothers if I set it off. Being the practical joker in the family, Tom rigged this one up from outside the bedroom, thinking one of his stooge brothers would trip it and get a good scare.

I stood there thinking, dang it, now what am I going to do?

The thought of trying to suppress the need to relieve myself seemed impossible, so I had to think quickly. I needed something to cut the string. I recalled that my tackle box had a pocket knife in it that I could use. I walked over to the box and, as I tried to open it, I found that it, too, had been rigged with one of these cursed devices. *What the heck? Really? Here too? Dang that Tom, he's thought of everything.*

I felt my bladder begin to tingle and cramp and decided that desperate times called for desperate measures. I would have to resort to relieving myself out the second-story window. I walked over to the window only to discover that it was also outfitted with a ladyfinger.

What, did he put these things everywhere?

I was a prisoner in my own room.

After mulling it over for a minute, I eventually gave up and went back to bed and tried to dream of deserts, salt flats, and camels. The next morning, I managed to find a way to cut the string. When I told Tom about my discomfort, he guffawed. I had to give it to him, he knew how to scheme a good practical joke. He was able to get into the mind of his younger brother and predict my path of escape rather succinctly. It might even be an eldest child superpower. Frankly, if I didn't think it was just a little funny myself, I would have been really ticked. It was a simple case of being the victim of our big family pecking order. When all was said and done, we both got a laugh out of it, so I was willing to forgive, but, evidently, not forget.

***

ROCK MUSIC WAS ALWAYS a big part of our family. The older siblings listened to the Beatles, Bread, and the Doors and subsequently passed down their musical influences to us younger kids. Most of us owned record players or stereos at one time or another growing up in the '70s. These units varied in quality from very cheap plastic with the built-in speaker to multi-component, high wattage stereos capable of shaking our bedroom windows. The Sony

Walkmans of the '80s were still years away and iPods were so inconceivable that they weren't even a crackpot thought. Nope, this was the era of albums, eight-tracks, and cassette tapes. Albums that skipped and popped, eight-tracks that switched channels mid-song, and tapes that were occasionally chewed by a hungry cassette player. While it got better with every technology leap, listening to music was still an imperfect science.

There was one particular phonograph of mine that was eventually passed down to Rob after I got my first stereo. It was a low-fidelity unit in every sense of the term, driven by a single tinny speaker and a stylus that had all of the engineering of a railroad spike when it dragged over records and butchered the music hidden within. With his hearing loss, Rob was no audiophile. He listened for pure pleasure and wasn't concerned with the proper mix of bass, treble, and mid-range. Even with his hearing aids, in order to hear the lyrics, he had to turn it up loud. This volume brought forth what little bass the underpowered phonograph was capable of, but was also the foundation of his listening enjoyment. He once explained to me how important the percussion section is to a deaf person. They like to *feel* their music, have it touch them, have it move them. It was always educational when Rob took me into the deaf world, the deaf culture. My hearing world was myopic at best, and growing up with him helped broaden my perspective.

He never had a lot of his own music. As a kid, I think he only had three 45 rpm records to his name. One of them was Kenny Rogers' "The Gambler," which he acquired in order to memorize the sign language lyrics for the song. His high school had a program called the Theater for the Deaf. This troupe put together a series of skits that were performed alongside various songs signed by the kids. Most of the kids were hard of hearing, so they relied on visual cues and pauses, as well as direction from their instructor in order to synchronize music and signs correctly.

In preparation for the production, he played the songs over and over and over again in his bedroom. The tinny sound of the phonograph speaker and the volume at which it was played made it impossible to escape if you were upstairs. Kenny's constant drawl and drone about the difference between holding up and folding up became the soundtrack to Rob's and the rest of our lives. The repetition, day after day, began to wear us siblings down. It is not the world's most uplifting song. Kenny's declaration mid-song that "the best that you can hope for is to die in your sleep" actually became kind of appealing. At least it would free us from the ongoing indecision of the conflicted Gambler.

But we were patient. Mom reminded us that Rob's hearing loss was as much a part of the family as he was. She continually told us that we needed to cut him some slack on the one song he really seemed to love. In line with Kenny himself, Mom was telling us that *we* needed to know when to hold up, as the song goes. Besides, we were all expecting the obsession with the song to end once the production was over. Of course, we were wrong. He continued playing the song for months after the play was over, but we all just rolled with it.

The same thing happened with another song that Rob had on a 45 rpm record, namely, Billy Joel's "Piano Man." He'd landed the lead in another skit by the Theater for the Deaf, and he made it his goal to nail the song. Behind the closed door, the phonograph spun and spun endlessly as Billy sang of tonic and gin as Rob waved his hands and contorted his fingers in synchronic elegant magnificence. He was in his element when he was signing. When he crossed over into the world of song, of song-sign, he immersed himself in a place of well-being and familiarity. The sadness of the song was overshadowed by the joy it brought to him whenever he played and signed it. Between the music of Joel and Rogers, it seemed that the plight of drinkers and gamblers set to music held a special place in Rob's heart.

Rob was a raging extrovert who also happened to love the spotlight. Because of this, when the time came to put on his production at the high school, he blew it out of the water. My mother, my sister Pat, and I all went and watched as he and his colleagues captivated the audience that night. During it, I saw how all the preparation that we endured over the weeks prior was finally paying off. As the gambler, he stood there in the spotlight in his cowboy hat with his Hollywood good looks and signed the song flawlessly. He had a natural stage presence and brought his best performance. There were several instances during the performance that tears welled up in me. He made me so stinking proud I wanted to stand up and say, "Yeah! That's my brother up there!" It was a stark reminder of how petty my grievances about the phonograph were. This was Rob's moment to shine, and he nailed it.

***

AFTER MY FEW YEARS OF SHARING a space with Rob and Paul, I was upgraded to my own room when Tom moved out of the house. Paul and Rob were happy to have me move on and enjoyed the added space. It was a better fit with just the two of them, like an odd couple of Oscar Madisons living together after Felix Unger moved out. It was always a mess. Clothes were strewn about like they'd been shot out of a leaf blower. School books were lost then found under beds—beds that were never made. There were games, toys, sports equipment, candy wrappers, occasional dishes, and the general unkemptness of boys. Mom didn't like going into that room. Between the two of them, the floor was never free from clutter and dirty clothes. Mom's preferred method of handling the unsightliness was to close the door. Out of sight, out of mind. She did, however, make it a point to vacuum every week on Saturday mornings, but only after nagging them to "clear the deck." It prevented the county hoarding staff from stapling health warnings on the door. In any case, I was ecstatic to finally have my own space and the two of them went on to be roommates until the next bedroom freed up.

It was the Portland Avenue boarding room wait list.

Chapter 5 - My Room

IN OUR HOUSE, GETTING YOUR OWN ROOM was a big deal. It meant you were old enough to move up the chain of independence to the point of being given something precious to any teen. Personal space. So when Tom moved out and Mom informed me, I was jazzed. Since I was an introverted loner, my room was my haven from the rest of the family. I'm pretty sure that's why God made doors, for kids like me to close them.

When it was determined that I would inherit Tom's room, Mom asked me what sort of décor I wanted. At the time, I was a huge Minnesota Vikings fan, so we went with purple and gold. My walls were a light shade of purple, with a dark purple bedspread and plush curtains with gold pullbacks. I accented it all with a Vikings pennant, fan buttons, and a few concert posters to shake it up a bit. My twin bed had a painted bookcase at the head stuffed with books, model cars, and a football autographed by the whole Viking team. The carpet was harvest-gold and complemented the motif quite well. Next to my bed was a cabinet that held my stereo, including turntable, tape deck, receiver, and a generous stack of LPs. On the wall next to my step-up closet stood my four-drawer dresser. It wasn't a huge room, but between the privacy factor and the ultra-cool football décor, I was happy as a kid could be. At least, until my room's décor took its first hit from a sibling.

One night in the early '70s, we were all called to the dinner table, as was the routine. Our kitchen was much cozier and less formal than our dining room, so it was where we ate our day-to-day meals. On this occasion, Mom prepared the usual fare of a meat entrée, a potato side dish, and a soggy canned vegetable of one color or another. It was most likely green or yellow waxed beans, a staple in our house in the '70s. For my first twenty years of life, I thought that was the only way vegetables were prepared—soft, mushy, and from a can. When I married, my wife introduced me to the concept of fresh or frozen vegetables. I wasn't aware that beans and other veggies should have a snap when you bite into them. Needless to say, I haven't eaten canned since.

We crowded around the table, each of us taking our chosen place. Rob, about eleven years old at the time, came to his seat late and seemed preoccupied and kind of edgy. Pat and Tom had both moved out by this time, so it was just the five of us, Mom, Jane, Rob, Paul, and me. Mom said the standard quick prayer that she always said at dinner time. "Bless us, Oh Lord, and these thy gifts which we are about to receive from thy bounty, through Christ, Our Lord. Amen." The words mean more now than they did then, but we were all taught the significance of thanking God that we were soon to have another meal under our belt.

We said our amens and the passing and reaching started. It was then Rob excused himself and said "I'll be right back." With a big family, this was a fairly common thing, so no one paid much attention. There was food to be eaten, and we were all hungry, so we kept passing and resumed our dinner. After a couple minutes of an empty chair, Mom finally asked, "Where is he?" It seemed a little suspicious and we were all beginning to wonder why he was gone.

He finally came through the kitchen doorway looking nervous and out of sorts. Once he sat down he kept wiggling in his chair and didn't establish eye contact with anyone. Mom had seen this act before on more than one occasion. There wasn't much that got past her when there was guilt to be had. After a few seconds, she inquired, "What exactly were you doing upstairs?"

"It's out," Rob answered.

"What's out? What do you mean?"

He looked at her, trying to feign a sense of calm. "Nothing. It was small, but it's out now."

It took Mom and the rest of us a couple of seconds to process what he was referring to. Based on a few other incidents with us kids and our fascination with playing with matches, she made an educated guess.

"Did you start a fire?" she asked, her voice taking on an interesting change in register and pitch. He nodded and she stood up quickly and headed for the stairs. The rest of us did the same, including Rob. After all, speaking from experience here, the only thing more exciting than the thrill of a fire was the tongue-lashing that someone would take for starting it. I've been on both the receiving and spectating end of these corrective soliloquies and, frankly, I would have preferred physical punishment. Mom didn't get mad and blow her top often, but when she did, she had a gift for scaring us straight.

We tromped up the stairs to assess the crime scene and witness Rob's arrest, trial, and sentencing. He led us to my room, a hard left at the top of the flight. We filed in and he opened my closet door to show the damage. The carpet had a fresh burn about the size of the palm of my hand. The burn was wet where he had doused it with water from the bathroom sink. There is nothing quite as permanent or as glaring on a floor as a carpet burn. Oh, you can cover it with a throw rug or a piece of furniture, but short of that, it's there. It's right there. The burn. That black spot right there. Yep, that's a burn, all right.

We all stood there and gawked at Rob's handiwork. I was upset he burned the carpet in my closet, but being a nonconfrontational kid, I figured he'd get punishment enough from Mom. He sure didn't need it from me. Besides, I had been in his situation before with a fairly sizeable closet fire I started in the Hubbard house, so I knew exactly how he felt. It seems as a family we had some sort of fascination with closet fires—closet pyromaniacs, if you will. There were a couple of gasps and a giggle from a few of us. Kids always seem to find a sadistic delight in a sibling's impending demise that causes them to titter like a bunch of monkeys in the peanut gallery.

"Robert Roy Landwehr, were you playing with matches?" Mom asked. Frankly, not many kids I knew used flint and steel to start their fires, but hey, it was always worth asking. It was Mom's attempt to amp up the public shaming a bit.

"Yes. I'm sorry, Mom," he said with remorse.

"You could have burned the house down." It was one of those timeless lines that parents have used with great effectiveness over the generations. I know it worked on me several years prior with the Hubbard incident—a fire that made his look like a cigarette burn in comparison. Yes, if you wanted a really good closet fire, I was your boy.

After a firm finger-shaking and furrowed-brow lecture from Mom, we all returned to the table to finish our dinner. The rest of the meal was much more subdued than usual. Anytime a scolding took place before supper, there was always a bit of tension in the air. Mom never held a grudge for long, and we all knew she loved us. Most of the time, she was just trying to keep us from killing each other through fire, electrocution, or other forms of involuntary manslaughter.

***

ONCE I HAD A ROOM OF MY OWN, I developed a new hobby building plastic models. It was a hobby that required concentration and solitude, both achievable inside the confines of my own room. I made it a practice to hoard my allowance for a number of weeks until I had the six dollars I needed to buy a model kit. Then on a Saturday morning, I boarded the number 3A bus on Grand Avenue and took it to Snelling Avenue. After a short wait, I'd transfer to the 84, which took me the rest of the way to the local Kmart. There was a great sense of freedom in doing this on my own. These kinds of cross-town bus trips were common back then and gave kids a confidence that helped us navigate life as adults.

At Kmart, I quickly found the model aisle amongst the other toys and scanned the shelves at the nearly endless possibilities of cars, planes, and ships. I usually ended up choosing a classic car from the '50s. Next I picked up any extra incidental supplies I might need as well, things like paint and citrus-scented model glue. There was much work to be done once I got home, making it easy to ignore the alluring call of the overhead announcements of momentary flashing blue light specials. "Attention Kmart shoppers, for the next fifteen minutes we will be running a special on foot baths in the housewares department under the flashing blue light." Foot baths? No, thank you. I had bigger fish to fry. This was serious business. Predictably, I got the usual sideways glance from the cashier when she rang up the glue, but I think she saw the rest of the modeling items and figured I was actually a hobbyist and not a kid looking to kill some brain cells. After paying, I bought a large cherry Icee for good measure, caught the bus, and headed for home.

When I got there, I immediately tromped upstairs to my bedroom and shut the door. I wanted to minimize all distractions and enter the world of my favorite hobby, a realm of focus and escape. This quiet solitude was my way of isolating and recharging my batteries after a week of school. It was just me, my model, and my clock radio. I started by spreading newspapers over my small desk in order to catch the paint spills, drips, and accidental glue squeezes. The desk was lit by a metal work light and a small lamp. I clicked the dial on the clock radio tuned to KDWB, one of the two local AM stations playing rock music in the Twin Cities at the time. From there, I consulted the instructions and gently broke the parts free from their molded plastic forms and began the assembly. It wasn't long before I lost myself in the meticulous work of assembling my model car. The instructions were simple and easy to follow to ensure any kid could do it.

Using a small amount of cement, glue part 1A to part 1B and allow to dry before painting.

These simple instructions were quickly violated. After all, I was twelve. Like an adult male trying to assemble a new piece of furniture, directions were looked upon more like guidelines for the weak-minded. On a regular basis, I applied a *liberal* amount of cement to part 1A, thereby creating a gooey mess. Furthermore, because model cement actually causes a chemical reaction which melts the plastic, it frequently melted the male end before it could be set into its female counterpart, 1B. I resorted to mashing the two together and holding them until they were stable. It ended up a little like bad virgin sex; disappointing at the beginning, but eventually after enough mashing together and some anxious moments, you figure it out. And frankly, when it was all done, you're just glad it's over with.

As I worked through assembling the pieces, first the engine, then the body, doors, hood, and trunk, I immersed myself in the world of plastic. All the while I was shrouded in a cloud of paint fumes and the chemically citrus smell of the contact cement. The citrus cover-up smell was the manufacturer's attempt to make a toxic product less noxious. I remember hearing of people sniffing glue to get high and thinking, well, that's pretty stupid. Needless to say, that thinking didn't prevent the clerk at the Kmart or the local drug store from looking over her glasses at me like I was some sort of grade school junkie every time I bought a tube. I think to make the same purchase today requires two forms of ID, a background check, and a note from your mother.

On an average of once an hour the song "Dream Weaver" by Gary Wright came on the radio. The song was hugely popular at the time and was played with great regularity on KDWB. Another hit was Aerosmith's "Dream On." Between these two songs and, perhaps, a tinge of help from the residual glue vapors, much of my assembly took on a dreamlike quality. It was certainly an altered state of consciousness for me. Even today, every time I hear "Dream Weaver," I am transported back to that room and the chemical smell of paint and cement.

After assembling the engine, I painted the hood and body and set them aside to dry. Eventually I moved onto the dreaded wheel assemblies, which were always made up of a tedious combination of a shock, struts, tie rods, wheels, springs, and hub caps. Because the wheels needed to pivot, as a way to mimic the turning of the steering wheel, their assembly was critical. On more than one occasion, I was heavy-handed with the glue and ended up melting something beyond recognition, thereby requiring that the front wheel be cauterized or hard-welded to the chassis. The result was a car with wheels that did not turn. Straight only. I tried to rationalize to myself.

Yeah, they make cars like that. I've seen 'em. They're rare, but I've seen "straight" cars. Sure.

It's unfortunate, but by the time it came to the finishing touches like the windshield, the final coats of paint, and applying the decals, my impatience was at its zenith. All of my earlier mistakes and snafus during construction compounded to create an urgent desire to finish and move on to the next project. Near the end of construction, if glue was applied too liberally I became careless and wiped it with an index finger rather than carefully using a toothpick. This inevitably led to glue from my fingertips ending up on the windshield, one of the most visible parts on a model. Another common mistake was mishandling the plastic decals, which seemed to take on a life of their own once they were off the sticky-backed paper. They flopped and stuck to everything within a two-foot radius, picking up bits of hair and dust in the process. These are the hack customizations you never see in the picture on the cover of the box. Look! Hairy decals! Of course, this was assuming they didn't tear in half entirely while I was taking them off the sheet, another source of considerable angst for a modeler trying to nail his presentation.

Other late-assembly, high-visibility errors like fingerprints on a not-quite-dry paint job or a wheel that didn't sit on the ground like the other three led to an internal explosive rage that made me want to hurl the whole plastic mess against the wall. It was a bit of the enraged artist coming forth. Sometimes it's the quiet kids you have to watch out for. We internalize the little things for so long that they begin to pile up like magma underneath a volcano. Every time, though, instead of lashing out in a rage, I took a deep breath and walked away for a bit. Looking back, these deep breaths were probably tainted with glue fumes, which might explain the resulting calmness. Perhaps I was a secondhand glue-sniffing junkie and I wasn't even aware of it.

Like any artist in the middle of a project, I never wanted people to see my work in progress. I preferred to show the finished product and let people marvel at my artistic genius. So, once the whole car was finished, I showed it around to my brothers, sisters, and Mom. They humored my dedication to the hermit-like nature of plastic car modeling with their oohs and ahhs and offered words of encouragement. They knew I was a kid who liked being alone for long periods of time, so this seemed like a natural fit for my personality. After showing my handiwork off, I put it on my bookcase shelf safely out of harm's way. There, it collected dust with the rest of my six-dollar creations.

I know model building was not a hobby for everyone—perhaps even boring to most people—but it taught me life skills like patience, planning, and problem solving. More importantly, it taught me that being alone is okay, and sometimes alone was where I was happiest. It provided countless hours for me just to sit and think. I can't imagine what I thought about at that age for those long stretches. Maybe the paper that was due in English class or an upcoming camping trip. Or perhaps a girl at school that I had a crush on. I don't know. I do know that as I fast forward forty years to this moment, where I sit typing this book on my laptop with my ear buds in, it makes me think maybe there's a cyclical pattern here. Once again I am alone, working on a project—a sometimes tedious one—and listening to music. This is my escape. It is where I am happiest.

***

DURING THE DATING YEARS between my mother and Jack, we periodically interacted with his eight children from his first marriage. By age, they were Kevin, Mary Pat, John, Patrick, Timmy, Maureen, Maggie, and Theresa. Maggie and Theresa were identical twins I could barely tell apart until Theresa cut her hair a little shorter. Our mother's dating pulled us into a relationship with Jack's children that was both strange and wonderful at the same time. Strange because at the time Jack's ex-wife, Mary, didn't want anything to do with the Landwehr kids. We were playing for the opponent's team in a manner of speaking, and we only served to remind her of his new relationship. Yet it was wonderful in that we suddenly had eight new stepsiblings, albeit living in their own house two blocks to the east on Portland Avenue.

Because the McKasy kids tried to honor their mother's wishes, they never spent much time at our house, and vice versa. However, on occasion, Jack did make it a point to mix us together for weekend trips to area beaches, as well as a few camping trips up north. I treasure those Saturdays Mom took us to Lake Owasso or to Bayport Beach with Jack and his kids as some of the best memories of summer. Usually Timmy, Maggie, and Theresa, all middle schoolers like us, came along and we'd have a day full of sun, sand, and barbeque. The other McKasy kids were either too old, disinterested, or preferred not to mix with us. It was during these outings that our relationship grew and flourished with our eventual stepfamily. We swam, fished, and threw the Frisbee around together. Timmy and I took turns catching football passes or fielding punts from Jack. When Jack tired, we tossed the football between ourselves or threw a softball with the twin girls. Later in the afternoon, Jack fired up the rickety three-legged grill and covered it with hamburgers and hot dogs. I always appreciated that he brought us together for these outings. Between the two families, the fourteen of us combined kids shared this common soul, Jack, who, while he had his issues, ultimately just wanted everyone to get along and truly loved all of us. These weekends together were proof of that.

Perhaps the most memorable night with the McKasy clan was the night they officially became our stepfamily. After nearly ten years of dating, my mom and Jack married in December of '79. They had a short ceremony at a local Catholic church, surrounded by their friends and the full gallery of us, their mutual children. After the ceremony, they took off to spend their honeymoon in beautiful downtown Hudson, Wisconsin. Word traveled quickly among the children and friends of both sides of the family that everyone was going back to our house on Portland for a spontaneous post-wedding reception blowout.

When I arrived back home from the church, Pat and Kevin, my new stepbrother, were sitting next to each other on the big couch in the living room. The two of them had begun dating a few months before Mom and Jack's wedding and by now had become an item. From a relational standpoint, it felt strange to me. We were, after all, stepsiblings to each other and, while there was no blood relation involved, it was a bit odd to see two stepsiblings dating. It seemed almost like incest-lite. Ironically enough, the two of them eventually married and are still married today. I referred to him as my stepbrother-in-law, which is actually what he was. After Mom and Jack divorced in 1985, he reverted back to being just a brother-in-law, and that's okay too.

I cannot claim total innocence from this interfamily attraction, though. Growing up as a middle schooler, I had my crushes on both of the twins and Maureen for a time. They were all attractive, athletic, and funny. My sister Jane had her boy-crush on Timmy as well. It seems there was some sort of twisted interfamily attraction across the board. I think if you asked any of us, each liked one or another boy or girl from the other family at some point. Being a shy kid, I never followed through on any of my attractions, mostly because it would have just been weird. Of course, all of these feelings and emotions were completely legitimate and expected given our hormonal rages at the time. But still. Weird.

As the evening wore on, Mom's big house steadily filled with people, cigarette smoke, and festivity. Kevin and others shouted out requests as I tended to Jack's stereo in the corner, spinning records from Eric Clapton, Jefferson Starship, and other favorites from the '70s. It was a happy occasion, a uniting of families that had been thrown together for ten years prior to Mom and Jack committing to one another. Everyone was in high spirits and the mood was upbeat and rowdy. Other wedding guests and friends of the family showed up wielding beer and bottles of brandy and rum, which were lined up on the kitchen counter. Throughout the night, toasts were raised to the happy couple. Later in the evening, as supplies dwindled and things got desperate, Jack's stash of cheap Canadian Club whiskey beneath the kitchen sink was pilfered. From there, the only place to go was down as low as his Blatz beer, which was always the signal of the end of any good party.

Like all good house parties, this one took on the appearance of a many-headed dragon. There were sub-parties that evolved and spun off from the main event. People clustered in groups of four or five and carried on lively conversations. Occasionally someone busted a dance move as they felt compelled. Riotous laughter like machine gun fire rang out over the music from time to time. It wasn't entirely unlike Pat's high school parties of a decade earlier, only an older more mature crowd. The whole scene was chaotic and filled with mayhem—a completely unorthodox, spontaneous celebration in the name of two people who weren't even present to enjoy it.

In the midst of the frothing living room party Maggie, Theresa, their girlfriend Amy and I went up into my room. The downstairs was getting crowded and we were all close in age so it made sense to make a party of our own. I had a kicking stereo and both the twins were music buffs, so the four of us crowded into my room. I let them browse through my LPs and when Maggie saw Neil Young's *Live Rust* album she said, "Oh good, you have Neil! Please, please put this on." It turned out they had seen Young in concert fairly recently, and had fallen in love with the album. I put the record on and we resumed talking, laughing, and drinking beer. A few songs into it, my friend Pat called. I mentioned we were having a house party and figured the more the merrier, so invited him. He knew the McKasys and was a great friend of mine who lived close, so he said he would be right over.

When he showed up, we both grabbed a beer and headed up to my room. Pat and I were eighteen and my stepsisters a couple of years younger. Maggie, still dressed in her wedding skirt and blouse, was beautiful with her feathered hair and slender figure. She was boisterously loud, fun, and quick with a one-liner. Theresa, the quieter of the two and with a shorter bob cut, was still wickedly funny and just as pretty as her twin sister. We were a bohemian gathering of teens on the precipice of the legal drinking age, nineteen at the time. After knowing these girls for so long, it was strangely satisfying laughing and drinking beer with them. We were growing up together and this night was serving, in some ways, as one of our rites of passage. For myself, I was just happy to be hanging with the cool kids, because my stepsisters were as cool as they come. They had only known me as a straight kid, the quiet Landwehr, so this occasion caught them off guard a bit, an interesting divergence from the norm.

As the evening wore on, we laughed and laughed. When our beers were drained, I made trips downstairs to get more. We talked about our schoolmates, rock concerts we had been to, and, most of all, about the shared childhood experience of having "Happy Jack" as a dad. His natural children affectionately called him this because of the fun-loving persona he took on when he'd been drinking. Despite his happy façade, none of us would deny Jack had a fairly serious alcohol problem through much of his life. His love for booze was ultimately the end to both of his marriages, his first to Mary Ann and his second to our mom, Mary Lou. Jack's issue was he never knew when to stop the party. Oftentimes, his drinking went overnight, which then led to the morning "hair of the dog," which devolved into a weekend bender. We all dreaded the benders because we never knew where he was or when he would turn up. Usually, he made his appearance early on Sunday afternoon to begin sobering up for the coming Monday dose of reality. He was what you might call a functional alcoholic, if there is such a thing. And yet, through all of this he was really the only dad I ever knew, and I loved him. Both of our families tried to love him the best we could. We repeatedly tried to love the disease out of him, to no avail.

When the album came to an end, I flipped it and played the other side. Young's electric guitar fired up and kept our little micro-party rocking. My friend Pat struck up a conversation on the side with the twins' friend and the two of them seemed to be hitting it off. I was having such a good time talking with the twins that I didn't want the night to end. As a recent graduate from an all-male military high school, I craved acceptance and attention from *any* girls, and if they were good-looking and related, well, that was even better. I wondered to myself whether they knew I had a crush on both of them and their sister Maureen. I figured they probably didn't so kept any sort of advance at bay so as not to freak them out. My feelings freaked *me* out enough without actually taking action on them. No sense messing up a great relationship because of some feelings that were probably not mutual. Of course, the desperate teen in me thought, if it was working for Pat and Kevin downstairs, maybe it could work for another couple of us.

Eventually, the party began to wind down. Around two a.m., I gave hugs to my twin stepsisters and wished them good night. My friend Pat got the phone number of Amy and went home as well. Looking back on this event, this celebration of our parents coming together, it's clear that it was pivotal in bringing us closer together as stepsiblings. Now that Mom and Jack were married, we were officially and undeniably relatives. We were on the cusp of young adulthood, and that evening our connections were redefined, both relationally and legally. Any lingering barriers that may have still existed crumbled down that night in my bedroom as Neil Young reminded us that it would take a lot of love or we wouldn't get very far. And, thirty years later, while Jack has passed on, his ex-wife Mary and her kids are as close to us as ever.

It seems we still have a lotta love.

Chapter 6 - Bathroom

WE HAD ONE BATHROOM IN OUR HOUSE. A mother, six kids, and one bathroom. Take a moment to let that sink in. To make matters worse, there was no shower in the bathroom, only a toilet, bathtub, sink, and medicine cabinet. This is really kind of astonishing when you think about it. How did we do it? My current home has only one bathroom, but there are only four of us living there and it has a shower. To help matters, we have a toilet in the basement. There is no sink, just a commode and four walls, but this emergency toilet has saved us from disaster or embarrassment numerous times. The thought of trying to orchestrate seven people getting ready for work or school with one bathroom is mind-numbing.

When we were young, as part of the scheduling, Mom designated Sunday night as bath night. This meant that usually two, but sometimes the three of us young boys would share a bath. It was a large tub, finished in the chosen color of most of the house, harvest-gold. She ran the water, then sent us in, let us undress and climb in and work out who was sitting where in the tub. We were allowed a few tub toys to encourage us to linger a while in an attempt to clean off the week's worth of kid-grime. As needed, we took occasional mid-week dunkings as well, but the only one that was mandatory was the Sunday night scrub-down. These affairs usually ended with a bad case of ring around the tub.

Amongst the bobbing tub toys, we goofed around, splashed, and even washed a little from time to time. It was never long before one of us managed to irritate one of the others to the point where we called for Mom. Exclamations of "Mom, he splashed me in the face!" or "Mom, he took my boat and won't give it back!" echoed off the walls and resonated down the stairway to the living room. Mom was usually downstairs enjoying a book or watching a television show. Sunday nights were her wind-down time where she rested and mentally geared up for another Monday morning and all the upheaval that goes with waking and readying six. When things got loud during Sunday bath night, she routinely called on The Enforcer, Tom, to take matters into his hands. This was never a good thing for us dirty little criminals in the bathtub. He usually showed up agitated that he'd been pulled from whatever he was doing to try to bring peace to our bathroom skirmish. His tactics were merciless, but effective.

He began by bursting into the bathroom and saying, "What is going on in here?" This was followed by an interrogation as to who did what to whom. The inquiry was strictly a formality, and any allegations carried little weight in the court of Tom's law. He simply needed a story in case Mom asked what was going on. After hearing us all out, he typically judged that everyone was equally guilty and thus all should be punished. He then took the water glass from the sink, filled it with cold water, and proceeded to give each of us a splash to the head or torso. Being in a tub of hot water made the shock of the cold feel like a kick in the chest. It also elicited screams and squeals from whoever caught the water flogging. It was an unconscionable abuse of power, but one that every big brother has the right to draw on in the name of peace and justice.

Of course, peace was the exact opposite of what came from the lighthearted water-boarding. We screamed loudly when the water hit while Tom laughed as he doled out our punishment one splash at a time. Try as we might to submerge as much of our bodies under the water, he always found the exposed skin and hit it. Once we stopped yelling, he laid down the law.

"Now, if you don't stop goofing around, I'm going to come up here and do this," and he delivered a bonus splash or two to drive the point home. It always meant more screaming, evasive submerging, and chaos. Of course, these gentle parting reminders were totally unnecessary, but Tom liked the big brother power trip. He was the bathtub cop turned Dirty Harry vigilante. *Now, I know what you're thinking, "Did he splash his cup empty or not? Feel lucky, punks?"* His tactics were unquestionably effective despite being an egregious abuse of the power and authority granted by Mom.

***

I CAME HOME AFTER A LONG DAY in sixth grade. As usual, I was eager to get changed into my play clothes and get outside. Tom was the only one home at the time and made it a point to meet me at the door. He had a serious look on his face as he spoke to me.

"Jimmy, the gas company called and they said that if we see anything suspicious in our water supply, like discoloration or anything, we are supposed to get out of the house. Apparently any discolored water contains some sort of poison gas, and could kill you. Just letting you know. Be careful."

Well, I wasn't going to let a poison threat slow me down from my time outdoors, so I went to my room and changed out of my school uniform. After I changed, I had to go to the bathroom so before I went downstairs, I made a stop in the bathroom. I was a bit tentative about Tom's warning, but before I started to go, the water was clear, so I was relieved to be able to pee without the immediate threat of death. Because no one wants to die in the bathroom.

When I was done, I flushed the toilet and, just as a precaution, watched as the bowl emptied. I was shocked when the bowl refilled with brown water. What the heck? Oh, no, it was happening! We were one of the houses with the poison gas!

"Tom! Tom! Brown water. It's the poison gas!" I shouted. In an effort to save myself, I covered my mouth and nose and turned and ran down the stairs, bounding them two at a time. Tom was waiting at the bottom of the stairs. "Hey, get out of the house, there's poison gas!"

"Oh, really?" he said as he reared back his head and broke into his sinister laugh. "It's poison gas. Ahhhhh!"

There it was. In my naiveté, I'd been taken again. Suckered by the elder, wiser sibling.

Evidently, earlier in the day we received a free sample of Sanka instant coffee in the mail. Tom thought it might better serve as the accelerant for a good practical joke on his kid brother. He showed me how he'd dumped it in the toilet tank and left it there for the next flush victim; in this case, it was me.

I guess it was a notch or two above death by poison gas.

***

I THINK OF OUR SINGLE BATHROOM for seven often when I am in modern-day homes, some with as many as four bathrooms. Along with serving its main purpose as a restroom, it was also the place where a sick kid went to lose his lunch, the location for multiple bathroom surgeries, and even the delousing station for a couple of lice outbreaks we brought home from school. The vanity mirror was where teenage acne was tended to, where '70s hair was blown dry to feathered perfection to look like Farrah Fawcett, and where metric tons of makeup were applied before school, work, or the homecoming dance. Its tub was one of the few havens in the house for an overburdened mother looking for a sanity-restoring soak. The sink served as the receptor of blood after the loss of a tooth or the flushing station for scrapes and open wounds. Yes, our bathroom was small, but mighty. And it not only taught us good lessons in sharing and waiting your turn, but also an appreciation for any house lucky enough to have more than one.

Chapter 7 - Other Bedrooms

THERE ARE A COUPLE OF BEDROOMS that do not hold nostalgia for me like the rest of the rooms in the house. I suppose this is the case in most every home. It is not a slight of the room itself, nor the fault of its occupants, just a matter of unconscious selective memory. My sisters Pat and Jane's room was one of them. I have very little recall of significant moments in their room. The only one that stands out was the night our dog Brandy gave birth to some pups. We knew she was pregnant for months and one summer night Jane and I heard some howling coming from upstairs. We followed the howling to the closet in her bedroom. When we got there, we found Brandy lying on her side in the middle of birthing a litter of pups. It was our first canine delivery, but we both surmised that we better assist her by breaking the amniotic sacs of the four puppies so they could breathe. The dog was too busy pushing out the next one to worry about tending to the last. They were beautiful black and white pups, a strange contrast to their mother's solid blonde coat. The black also tipped us off as to the color of her unknown suitor.

Other than that isolated event, there is nothing much to reflect on with regard to their room. For a number of years, both of my sisters shared the space, pretty much making it the *Temple of Doom* to my brothers and me. It was enter at your own risk and we all knew it. My sisters were gifted at striking fear into the hearts of us boys and we had a healthy fear of their wrath. Being in a four-to-two minority, they needed to operate from a platform of fear and intimidation to keep us out of their space. There was nothing much of interest to us in there

69

anyways, save for an occasional record album worth borrowing. So we kept our distance.

The other room that falls off the nostalgia train was Mom's. Other than serving her breakfast in bed on Mother's Day and maybe the famous photo album-browsing bacon fire incident, I can't recall any captivating moments in her room. I do know it was her decompression chamber and that when the door was closed, you could still knock and enter, but you'd better have a really good reason. Mom needed her rest and was usually in bed by ten o'clock. For the most part, when she was sleeping it was best to try to stave off any bleeding or splint any broken bones you might have until morning. She'd bandage you either way, but in the morning she might even do it with a smile on her face.

It is my guess Mom had her share of fretful, sleepless nights in that bedroom. Nights spent worrying about how she was going to pay for the car repair, the electric bill, or the next set of orthodontics inevitably coming down the pike. Perhaps some nights spent crying about the crushing weight of single parenthood, the uncertainty of tomorrow, or worry over the path one of us was heading down. I suspect there were a whole lot of prayers uttered to Jesus, the Virgin Mary, and all the Saints, as well. Mom always had a deep faith and I am a firm believer in the fact that these prayers helped pull us through. The fact that our family navigated those years of single parenthood with nary a felon or serial killer in the bunch, well, it's kind of proof of the power of prayer, itself.

I don't know what to make of the lack of recall for these two rooms. They fall into the "black hole" category for me. Mom always said there were black hole years when she was raising us. These were years when, after one of us recounted a story from our youth, she'd say, "I have no memory of that at all. It must have been during the black hole years." So it seems we *all* lost some things during those days in the '70s. I will say that these two rooms were functionally as important to the whole as the rest of them. They were refuges for the women of the house, who, more often than not, were responsible for keeping the whole thing afloat, the ship on course. If I may beg a political analogy, it was almost as if Mom's room was the oval office and the sisters' the war room. Together, the list of executive orders and negotiating directives coming from them served as a system of checks and balances to make sure the tiny country of Portland was running smooth.

Chapter 8 - Attic

OUR HOUSE FEATURED A FULL WALK-IN third-floor attic. It was poorly lit, drafty, and dusty; hot in the summer and cold in the winter. As attics go, it was spacious and expansive. There was an unfinished wood floor covering the six inches of cellulose insulation, sorely inadequate given the harshness of Minnesota winters. The space served mainly as a storage area for Christmas decorations, boxes of old photos, collectibles, and nostalgic items like Mom's wedding dress or the little girl purse of my deceased sister, Linda. It was not a place any of us wanted to spend much time in because, well, everyone knows that if ghosts are to be had, they're likely in the attic.

Tales of the Portland Avenue house being haunted are, in large part, unfounded and undocumented. Most of them were either started or perpetuated by Pat, a lifelong believer and promoter of the paranormal. She purports she had a handful of encounters with ghosts in the houses we lived in and was always a believer in UFOs as well. For example, before we moved to the Portland house, at a young age, Pat sighted a UFO while running for milk at the local grocery store. When she returned home, she showed the strange lights in the sky to our mother. Mom clarified to her that it was only a set of spotlights for a local store's grand opening. Then, years later at the Portland house, both she and Mom sighted a football-field-sized spaceship hovering over St. Luke's Church. Oddly enough, this sighting never made the news, but seemed to gird up the foundation for Pat's obsession with all things unseen by the rest of us kids. Had we lived there longer, I've little doubt that Sasquatch and Goatman would have made an appearance.

Despite my cynicism, it is impossible to deny that there were occasions when strange, inexplicable events took place. One night in the early '80s as my mother and stepfather were sleeping, Jack got up and, without explanation, went downstairs to sleep on the couch. After he left, as Mom tried to get back to sleep, she heard footfalls going up the stairs to the attic. It struck her as unusual because she knew Jack wouldn't go up there, nor would anyone else at that time of night. As she lay there speculating about the footsteps, she heard what sounded like furniture being moved overhead. She finally got out of bed and called up the stairs, "Hey, who's up there?" There was no response. Befuddled, she went back to bed and eventually fell back to sleep.

The next morning, Mom asked Jack why he had gotten up and where he went. He said he'd slept on the couch. "I couldn't sleep because of all the racket in the attic," he said. My mom said his statement made her go cold. She couldn't believe her ears. He'd heard the same noises coming from the attic that she had, enough so to drive him downstairs to escape it. It was proof she had not imagined it all and gave additional validity to the strange event. When trying to rationalize what had happened, my mom first had to rule out that it was one of us kids. Oddly enough, we were all accounted for, either in our beds, or spending the night at a friend's house. Furthermore, the attic was such an uninviting place, most of us never ventured up there in broad daylight, so doing so at night was almost unspeakable. There was simply no logical explanation for the noise from above. When she told me the story, I got a little creeped out. While all the rest of the haunted house stories were experienced by a single person, here was a case where two people heard the same thing. And while it wasn't an official ghost sighting, the circumstances around it didn't help to disprove the creepy haunting lore that had been building over the years. If one had to prove whether or not Portland was haunted, this occurrence surely left the book open.

***

THE INFAMOUS ATTIC/STAIRWAY INCIDENT served to fuel a paranormal investigation, or a sad parody of one, a couple of years later. It took place on the evening of one of my annual Tribute to George Thorogood parties. It was late and the party had whittled down to a few of my buddies and my brother Rob. We were all in the kitchen and approaching the silly stage from too much keg beer while Thorogood's "House of Blue Lights" blasted on the stereo in the living room. Somehow the conversation drifted to telling my friends Ross, Chris, Bear, and Gary about the theories that the house was haunted.

"Yeah, some weird stuff's been happening lately. We think there might be a ghost living among us."

"Yeah? Like what kind of stuff?" Chris inquired.

"Just little stuff, like finding the water running in the bathroom or the kitchen. Oh, and one time my mom and stepfather heard footsteps in the attic, even though it was none of us." I filled them in on the details of my parents' weird experience. Rob nodded his agreement and backed up my stories.

"I've nicknamed her Elsie Mae," I said in jest. I was cynical, but my friends seemed intrigued, so I thought I'd play it up a bit.

Suddenly, Chris perked up and exclaimed, "A séance!"

"What, now?" I asked, surprised at the far-out suggestion.

"Yeah, now! Let's see if this is for real."

Chris was as skeptical as the rest of us but also had a wicked sense of humor. It was getting late and we were all looking for a diversion, so his suggestion actually sounded like a nice change from drinking beer out of a measuring cup, which seemed to happen at every good party.

Everyone knows all good séances require a candle, so I went and pulled one out from the dining room buffet drawer. "Follow me," I said as I led the entourage up to the second floor. At the top of the stairs was the attic door. When I started up the stairs with my friends close behind, the smell of our attic hit me in the face. It smelled of dust and cellulose; of decaying paper and wood planking. It was a smell that immediately brought to mind unfashionable clothes and memories stuffed into cardboard boxes—a past that only came to life with the opening of that door. We were going back in time to find someone whose existence I doubted, but somehow, the attic seemed like the most logical place to look.

I flicked on the switch, lighting the lone bulb that served as the only source of illumination. We marched up the dozen steps of the staircase, the walls on either side covered with brown spray paint and fluorescent graffiti. Years ago, Tom and Pat made the attic into a bedroom/hangout space for the summer months and, as part of their hippie-ness, spray painted the stairwell. It was a '70s free-expression canvas waiting to happen. They doodled in hideous, dirt-brown spray paint with swirls and geometric shapes and then augmented it with hand-painted fluorescent peace signs, flowers, and sayings of the day. When it was done, it was no worse looking than before and actually gave the stairwell some much-needed character. Unless you weren't a fan of the whole hippie movement, in which case it was probably just shocking.

My friend Chris seemed to be the séance ringleader, partly because it was his suggestion, but mostly because he thought it would be a good chance to be the head clown for this paranormal circus. I lit the candle, melted a little wax into a puddle on the rough floor, and stuck the candle into the warm wax mush. When I switched off the light, Chris took over from there.

"Okay, everyone, get in a circle around the candle and join your hands cross-ways," he ordered.

"Does cross-ways make it better somehow?" I asked quizzically.

"Of course, all good séances do it cross-ways," he answered with conviction as he struggled to keep a straight face. A few in the circle snickered, an undertone which kept the mood light. It was apparent this was going to be like *Dark Shadows* meets *Animal House*. Each of us complied, crossed arms and joined hands with the person on either side.

"You guys, be quiet now. I'm trying to reach the fourth dimension," Chris continued.

"Try more beer," Bear said.

This brought forth more laughter and disruption. "Very funny, Bear. C'mon, be serious. We gotta channel Elsie Mae!" Chris pleaded.

Eventually we settled down, allowing Chris to pick up where he'd left off.

"Elsie Mae, we come in peace."

Just then a fart rang out and the monkey business started all over again. It became clear that Elsie Mae was competing with Bluto and the gang, for sure. If we were successful in reaching her, it was clear she better have a sense of humor, or we were all done for.

After a couple more false starts, Chris resumed and regained control of his attempted mediumship. "Elsie Mae, we come in peace. If you are with us, give us a sign," Chris said in his best scary séance voice. We sat there waiting. The candle suddenly fluttered in a disrupted way, the handiwork of someone in the circle with a good set of lungs and an apparent disrespect for the undead.

Chris gasped and said, "Look! It's a sign!" trying to build the excitement of the moment a bit more.

"Okay, who did that? Was that you, Ross?" I asked.

"Who, me? Never." No one admitted to being the wind behind the candle flicker, but the cynicism in the confines of the attic was certainly much larger and more imposing than any ghost, that much was sure. The giggling and messing around continued for a minute or two before Chris called us all back to order again. "Hey, guys, c'mon. I think she's with us," he said with salted sarcasm. As a conduit to the nether-side, his efforts were shrouded in barley, hops, and twenty-something nonsense. He failed to manufacture fear or suspense among us, his inebriated congregants. Our scorn and mocking only served to egg him on, knowing he had the spotlight on the epitome of how to un-channel a spirit.

He restarted his feeble channeling attempts. "Elsie, where are you right now?"

At that moment, the candle flickered and went out. A couple people screamed sarcastically, causing more laughter in the circle. I yelled, "I want my mom!" Ross shouted the line from the *Monty Python and the Holy Grail* movie, "Run away, run away!"

Everyone stood up in the now pitch-black room and headed toward the stairs. It was apparent to all that this séance was over in favor of getting back to the keg. Though none of us experienced anything at the séance, it was obvious that lingering in a dark place with a history of creepy happenings was something nobody necessarily wanted to press, either. We hurried down the stairs and reconvened in the kitchen. People filled their cups and we recapped the event.

"That was scary. Or not," Ross said.

"Yeah, I think Elsie Mae has a breathing problem," I joked.

Chris took a sip of his beer, smirked, and said sarcastically, "Didn't you all feel the energy?"

"Nope. Unless you count the fart. I think we all felt that," Bear replied.

We all laughed and before long got back to talking about music, work, and school. It seemed that the poltergeist in the attic was either shy, or didn't exist after all. And, though I was never comfortable messing around with the supernatural, the séance served to sort of prove that there was nothing to worry about.

Or so I thought at the time.

After the party cleared out, Rob and I cleaned up for a bit and then headed to our rooms to go to bed. As I lay there trying to get to sleep, I heard a thud on the wall of my room. It was loud and caused me to sit bolt upright. What the heck? I began to wonder if we had riled something up with our derisive séance. Maybe we shouldn't have stirred still waters. The strange noise was a bit too coincidental and, frankly, I was a terrified.

I opened my bedroom door and started down the steps. If I heard right, the noise came from the wall along the staircase. I walked down to the landing and stopped in my tracks. Lying there before me was my framed high school picture. All of my siblings' portraits still hung on the wall, completely unaffected. A shiver went up my spine. Well, *this* is disturbing, I thought. After all, Rob's picture was undisturbed, and he'd been at the séance. Apparently, Elsie Mae was selective about who was to be the victim of her haunting. Tonight, for good reason, it seemed to be me.

I hung the picture and went into Rob's room and told him to come out into the hallway. When I explained what happened, he raised his eyebrows in shock. Because of his hearing loss, he had not heard the noise at all, but was creeped out when I told him. Paul, the only other sibling living in the house at the time, was not home yet, so it couldn't have been him. After a couple of minutes and an agreement that the incident was weird, Rob just said, "Well, goodnight. I'm glad it wasn't *my* picture. Sleep well, bro!" and, with a laugh, went back to bed.

Needless to say, it took me a while to drift off that night.

About a month later, Rob, Gary, and I were at our house getting ready to go out for the night. I told Gary about what happened after our séance.

"Yeah, and the creepiest part of the whole thing was that only *my* picture was off the wall," I said, still a bit unnerved about the incident.

"Really? That's so weird." He looked at me seriously for a few seconds before he broke into a guilty grin. Then he started laughing and said, "That was me. I did the whole thing. I came back in your front door, banged on the wall, and put your picture on the landing."

Rob and I laughed, realizing we'd been had. Evidently, on the night of the party, Rob and I left the front door unlocked for Paul, and Gary took advantage of it to give me a good scare. He, too, was a cynic and was out to prove a point. It was an expertly conducted prank and I had to give him credit. I had been duped into thinking Elsie Mae had it in for me and only me. In the end, I was grateful to find out it was only a joke. It had been an unsettling month. Needless to say, I haven't participated in a séance since.

***

THERE WERE A COUPLE OF OTHER CREEPY incidents during my years on Portland. The first came when I was home from school making my lunch one day. Students were allowed to go home, and since we lived right across the street, I occasionally ate there to change things up. On this day, as was my routine, I got a pot from below the stove and opened a can of Chef Boyardee Ravioli and dug it out with a spoon. I twisted the knob on the stove and as I turned to put my fork in the sink, two Tupperware lids fell out of the cupboard that was open to my right.

I froze. Pat's and Jane's tales of how the house was haunted and their allegations of mystical mayhem quickly replayed in my head. In the past, I usually dismissed them as crackpot accounts of my two superstitious sisters. Why was it that they always saw the action and never me? I always doubted them with a skeptical curiosity, until now.

As I stood there with a fork, looking at the lids lying on the counter, I suddenly realized how alone I was in the big house. Or maybe I wasn't? Perhaps I should be setting a table for two today. I also noticed how eerily quiet the house was. Just me and my overactive imagination. I tried to divert my thoughts away from the fact that the ghost I didn't want to acknowledge was having trouble finding the right container in the cupboard.

Think happy thoughts. Happy thoughts.

I waited for a few seconds just to see if anything else odd happened while I was ready to witness. Nothing but silence. A deafening silence.

Deciding that I had about enough eeriness for the moment, I walked out to the living room and put my sister's Elton John album on the old cherry wood stereo console. I cranked it up loud, because every kid knows ghosts are afraid of noise, right? That was my thinking anyway. Nothing a little "Saturday Night's Alright for Fighting" at high volume won't scare off. If I couldn't scare them off, I could at least make their luminescent ears bleed.

The music seemed to do the trick, as I didn't have any further interruptions that day. This is not to say that the whole ordeal was not a purely coincidental happening. Maybe the lids were precariously perched in the cupboard to begin with. Or perhaps I bumped them when I opened the cupboard earlier and moved things just enough to make the lids fall out unexpectedly minutes later. Both options sounded convincing enough for me and were the story I was going to hold to, at least until I finished lunch and started on my way back to school.

The other creepy incident took place years later during my college years, when I was in my room reading a textbook about Meso-American history. I sat on my bed, with my door cracked open about a foot or so, when suddenly I had the distinct feeling I was being watched by someone at the door's opening, an unnerving perception that there were prying eyes I could not see. It was a terribly disturbing and violating sensation, one that I'd never had before. There was clearly a presence of some sort in the room with me. Someone uninvited. Someone I did not know.

As I began trying to rationalize my irrational thoughts and perceptions, a breeze blew past me. A chill went up my back and the hair on my arms stood up. Okay, what was that? I'm out! I knew that to maintain my sanity I needed to get out of my room. I got up, slowly walked to the door, then bolted down the stairs two at a time. When I had a chance to regroup, I fully recognized that the whole event was probably more my overactive imagination taking control than anything paranormal. At the same time, I also knew I wasn't crazy about sharing my room with anyone but the long-dead Meso-Americans inside my book. Furthermore, if it *was* some supernatural being, it was clear that it was not confined just to our attic. It liked to get out and roam a little.

***

GROWING UP, I WAS AN INNOCENT and always very trusting of people. I took them at their word and assumed the best of them. I trusted their motives were pure. While I liked to think of myself as an innocent, others might have less redeeming words for this quality. Words like gullible, or sucker, or naive. My brother Tom knew of these tendencies and decided to capitalize on them. He knew of all the alleged haunting stories around the house and was always quick to prey on his siblings' weaknesses in the name of a good practical joke. We all took it in stride. We had to. In our house of lowland gorillas, he was the Silverback.

When I was about fifteen, I was deep into reading the bestseller *The Amityville Horror*. It is a novel based on a true story of a family that moves into a house where a man murdered six of his family members a year earlier. All sorts of strange things started happening shortly after this family moved in. The story is fairly graphic, describing things like swarms of flies in the house in the dead of winter, blood oozing from walls, random door slamming, and other bone-chilling events. It even described a crucifix that was inexplicably turned upside down.

I struggled through the book. I tend to scare easily and many parts of it had me too frightened to turn the pages. Reading it alone in my room was nearly impossible. As a way of working it out, I told various members of the family some of the details as I progressed through it. It seemed helpful to share some of the creepiness with them. The facts that the story was allegedly true and that we had some strange happenings around our house and Pat's insistence that Portland was haunted made it even harder not to be freaked out.

Suffice it to say, all of these things combined to make me a nervous wreck while I was reading it.

One evening I walked into my room and found my crucifix hanging upside down on my wall. I was instantly panic-stricken. How did this happen? It's just like in the book! I knew I shouldn't be reading this stuff—flirting with the spirit realms. This story is starting to freak me out! I was living in my own Portland Avenue Horror.

I ran downstairs all wide-eyed and told Tom, "My crucifix was hanging upside down, just like in *The Amityville Horror*!"

To which Tom replied, "Really? Did you see any flies or blood?" Then he cocked his head back and laughed riotously.

In my innocence, I'd been taken for a fool. And, frankly, I was a little glad for it.

I should have suspected he was behind the prank the whole time. Tom was skeptical of all things paranormal. He not only thought things like that were ridiculous, he thought the people who believed in them were ridiculous too. Playing tricks like the inverted crucifix on suckers like me gave him the chance to disprove our theories and show us how silly we were at the same time. In this case, it worked quite well. I felt duped by his trick and dumb for placing that much credibility in a book in the first place. Nevertheless, I stopped reading it shortly thereafter and never did finish it.

One can never be too sure.

***

SMOKING WAS MUCH MORE CULTURALLY accepted during the '70s. I remember seeing cigarette commercials on television before they were outlawed. Doral's "Taste me, taste me" jingle still runs through my head at times, even though I've never tasted one. Camel's slogan of "I'd walk a mile for a Camel" is still one of those catchy phrases I can't seem to forget. Most smokers I know won't walk down the block to get a pack, let alone a mile. Furthermore, if they'd walk that mile, in their breathlessness, they might even be convinced to quit. Those icons of the '70s we worshipped, including the rugged, leather-skinned Marlboro Man and the sassy liberated woman smoking Virginia Slims, made the bad habit look cool.

Mom started in her early teens and smoked her whole life. Her habit meant my siblings and I all grew up around it. One of my youngest memories was of lying in bed with Mom one night when I couldn't sleep. I lay there watching the ember of her cigarette in the darkness and smelling the comforting, albeit noxious, secondhand smoke of her Alpine cancer stick. I find it a bit ironic they would name a cigarette after a thin-air environment that causes shortness of breath, but I digress. My guess is she was probably using it to help her relax so she could get to sleep. Like many smokers, it seemed to calm her anxieties about the future or pressing issues. The habit took the edge off. This was a unique occurrence because, as a rule, she didn't usually smoke in bed.

Along with the habit came an ashtray in almost every room of the house. They took different shapes and forms; deep, shallow, ornate, ugly, round, square, and oval, we had them all. They sat on coffee tables, end tables, buffets, and countertops awaiting the remnants of someone else's vice. Author Kurt Vonnegut once said, "The public health authorities never mention the main reason many Americans have for smoking heavily, which is that smoking is a fairly sure, fairly honorable form of suicide." I always thought that was a poignant description of a smoker's experience. There is an element of self-loathing that goes along with lighting up, I think. People have known the perils of puffing for years yet they still do it. Despite the government's attempt to regulate and tax it out of existence, people still like to draw toxins into their bodies in the name of relaxation. Though it's not for me, I totally understand the need for people to control their own lives. If sucking on a 'grit gives them five minutes of sanity in a world full of chaos, well, then go for it.

Because my mom and stepfather were both lifelong smokers, our house always had a tinge of acrid smell to it. The same held true for the car. There was never much thought given to secondhand smoke back then. Smoking was perfectly acceptable done indoors and in vehicles. It was an accepted habit, like it or not. On several occasions, we hid Mom's cigarettes in the effort to make her quit. "Where are my cigarettes? Who hid my cigarettes?" she asked. Inevitably, one of us fessed up and pulled them out of hiding. In her defense, Mom did try quitting a number of times over the years, with limited success. Her method of stopping cold-turkey usually lasted only a few weeks. Then, after gaining a few pounds or in the face of a stressful event, she'd surrender and borrow one from someone, or dig a pack out of hiding. All it took was one and she'd be back on the half-pack-a-day habit that kept her going day-to-day. I never begrudged her the habit. If I was a single parent of six, I'd probably reach for something myself, most likely an amber-colored liquid with a high proof. Cigarettes helped her cope.

My sister Pat was the first of us kids to take up smoking. Like many kids of that era, she started as a teenager to be cool. I discovered her habit one night when she was about seventeen. She took me and Jane with her to hang out with a few of her friends near St. Agnes High School. She was supposed to be watching us and the only way to get to hang out with her friends was by telling Mom we were going to a movie. We walked to the school where she met a few of her girlfriends and a couple of boys and they all goofed off, smoked, and listened to the radio on the steps of a nearby playground building. It was harmless teenage fun, but I can remember worrying about how much trouble she would get in if she were caught puffing at her young age. I was a self-righteous, paranoid eleven-year-old so most of it was unwarranted worry. But that was how I operated, Saint James the Pious.

Pat somehow kept her smoking a secret from Mom despite the fact Tom, Jane, and I all knew. In an effort to build her alliance, she resorted to a bit of blackmail one day while Mom was at work. Tom was home and Rob and Paul were playing outside somewhere. Jane was thirteen and I twelve when Pat secretly told us to go up in the attic with her. She claimed there was something she wanted to show us. We followed her up the staircase into the musty attic. "Sit down on the floor over here," she said. Jane and I sat cross-legged on an old rug. I wondered where all the secrecy and mystery was leading. It wasn't like Pat to fully engage us kids for any length of time, let alone two of us together. I was beginning to smell a rat.

Pat pulled out a pack of Marlboro reds and a book of matches. Jane and I both kind of gulped and looked at each other in shock. "You guys, we're going to smoke, okay?" Pat said, more telling than asking.

"Uh, okay . . ." we answered.

"If you wanna be cool, you've got to know how to do it right.

"First you light it." She put the cigarette in her lips, struck the match, and lit it. The end flamed up as the cigarette started to glow. It was a familiar sequence we had seen hundreds of times before with our mom, except she used disposable lighters.

"Then you suck it in; all the way into your lungs, not just your cheeks. You've got to inhale or else you're just faking it. And everyone can tell if you're faking," she warned.

Now, I'd seen and heard enough anti-smoking propaganda at school to know what we were embarking on was likely an instant ticket to an early grave. I remember one demonstration in class that showed a mason jar filled with white cotton next to another filled with tar-stained cotton. As students, we were told our lungs would certainly look as bad as the second jar if we took up the habit for any significant length of time. It was a simplistic scare tactic, but extremely impactful. It was enough to convince me that while I might go along with the dirty deed we were about to undergo, I would almost certainly never take the habit up of my own free will.

She passed the cigarette to Jane and said, "Here, take a drag." She explained that a drag was the hip term for inhaling deeply. Jane took it, looking uncomfortable and unsure of how to hold it. She looked as if she was holding a stick of dynamite or a scorpion—not quite sure whether to throw it or inhale it. She pursed her lips and took a puff and let out a couple of short coughs. Pat chuckled and explained that everyone coughed a bit their first time. The habit wasn't quite as glamorous as they showed in the TV commercials; that much was apparent.

"Jimmy, it's your turn now," Pat said. Jane passed the burning cigarette to me. I knew taking a puff was so much the wrong thing for a kid my age to do. I didn't want to be there. I was in a den of innocence-lost and there was no way out. I was practically losing my smoking virginity against my will. More than anything, I was worried about getting in trouble with Mom. I feared not only of disappointing her, but also how it would look to other siblings and friends if and when they found out. Prison time wasn't likely, but in my mind, it would be just short of it.

I took the cigarette as the push of peer pressure outweighed the pull of my righteousness. What the heck, I was always the good kid and this would prove to my sisters that I was capable of being a cool hippie punk too. I took a short drag off the cig and held it in my cheeks for a few seconds. The smoke burned my nostrils and throat. I blew it out more as an act of rejection than release. Like Jane, I finished the whole exercise off in a coughing fit. How could anyone enjoy something so physically offensive? I wondered. With the possible exception of looking cool, which I am certain at the age of eleven I did not, there was nothing pleasurable about it. Maybe it took a few puffs to get it right, to figure out how to enjoy it.

I passed it back to Pat, who took a drag. She engaged the cigarette with such ease and cool. Unlike Jane and I, who were only gargling with the smoke, choosing not to swallow, she clearly took it into her lungs and seemed to enjoy it. It was obvious she had considerable practice at this and we were amateurs in the presence of nicotine-ingesting greatness. We passed it around again. Jane took a second drag and managed to cough a little less, or at least stifle it with style. I did the same, trying this time to fully inhale, but only succeeded in getting another cheek full of smoke. I launched into another coughing fit as the smoke had its way with me. Between the cigarette and me, I wasn't sure who was smoking who, at that point.

"You have to suck on it like you're sucking through a straw," Pat said. I was past the point of wanting advice on how to make this process something that could be enjoyed. Like the smoke in my cheeks, I wanted out. This sucked. It didn't help that in my eleven-year-old mind it was a sinister act of depravity. I was convinced it was the on-ramp to harder vices like drinking beer and staying up past midnight. I wanted the whole thing over with, before Mom or someone else in my family found out.

We passed it around until it was gone. Pat snubbed it out in an ashtray and proceeded to disclose the binding terms of the previously undisclosed contract. "Okay, now that you guys have smoked, you can never tell Mom that I do."

"Uh, okay," I said. It was all I could come up with after having been bamboozled so definitively by my cunning older sister. Blackmailed! We'd been blackmailed by our own flesh and blood! I should have known all along there was a motive behind this clandestine meeting. It was not simply an attempt to bond with her siblings, but rather a way of covering her own backside.

Pat put the ashtray back into hiding and we headed down the attic stairs. When we got to the bottom, everyone went their own direction. I started toward the bathroom to brush my teeth when I heard Tom call from his bedroom, "Jimmy, come here." My heart dropped. Oh no! This was it, for sure. I was about to be found out, followed by a certain conviction and sentencing. My shoulders slumped and I sulked into his room.

"Let me smell your breath." I opened my mouth and blew my tar-laden breath into his face.

"Uh-huh. Just as I suspected," he said, dismissing me.

I left the room thinking, *Oh my God. This was it. I was dead.*

Just for good measure, I went to the bathroom and brushed my teeth vigorously. I spent the rest of the afternoon worrying about the wrath of Mom that would surely rain down on me if Tom told her. If the "good kid" in the family couldn't be trusted, who could? I was sure to be a disappointment to her.

As fate would have it, Tom's intention all along was simply to give me a good scare. He never told Mom. It's my guess he figured I would do more to punish myself over time than our mother ever could, and he was spot-on with that assumption. I worried about being found out for months afterward. But fortunately for me, this was a case of a sibling taking the high road in the name of watching out for his little brother. What happened in the attic, stayed in the attic.

And I never even thanked him for that.

Chapter 9 - Basement

OUR BASEMENT WAS UTILITARIAN and simplistic. It was certainly nothing worth putting any money or work into remodeling. The floors were painted battleship gray and the cinder block walls were lined with a skim coat of plaster. The plaster bubbled up the size of baseballs in some places and my brothers and I discovered that when you smashed these, it sent the plaster falling to the floor and usually released a centipede that skittered away, which we took great delight in stomping.

These were simpler times.

I'm certain had she known about our antics, Mom would not have approved of us creating plaster divots in her wall in the pursuit of a little mindless fun.

Four strong, square pillars holding up the first floor were aligned in a row down the center length of the basement. At the far end of the room, our boiler hulked like an oversized furnace troll. Cloaked in asbestos, it created the steam that provided the moist, radiant heat to the house. Despite its prehistoric appearance, it functioned well for us over the years. That's not to say there weren't occasions when the pilot light went out and either Mom or one of us kids were required to risk burning the hair off our fingers during a relight. I remember being assigned the task at the beginning of one heating season and fearing for my life. To a kid, it felt like I was lighting the fuse to a

Saturn V rocket. I always feared she'd blow and the whole house would go up in a mushroom cloud, but she never did. Just a hiss, a whoosh, and the boil was started.

Next to the furnace stood our water heater. Undersized at thirty gallons, it was perpetually overworked with the seven of us constantly taxing it, taking it from full to empty in a single bath. Hanging above the water heater was a large vent which allowed the carbon monoxide to escape up and out through the chimney. At some point in time the vent became unhooked. During an annual boiler inspection, the technician noticed the misaligned vent. He asked Mom how long it had been like that. She said she had no idea. He then told her what its function was and of the dangers of carbon dioxide buildup—how it was a silent killer. When she heard this, her jaw dropped. At the time, Tom had his bedroom in the basement and Mom quickly realized how close we came to a tragedy. We dodged a bullet.

On the far wall, next to the washing machine, stood a couple of cast iron dump-sinks. The washer's black rubber outlet hose with its lint screen attached dumped directly into these. As the lint screen clogged up over time, water squirted out in a dozen different directions and eventually the machine emptied and the drain water crested just inches from the top of the tub. I remember watching the water level rise up the side and fearing that the main sink would overflow. It was a spectator sport for the bored.

As I said, it was a simpler time.

In the early 1980s, Tom built a shower stall in the corner near the washing machine. He did an admirable construction job given the confines he had to work within. The whole enclosure was built on a raised platform to allow clearance for the drainage pipe which ran down a length of PVC and directly into the exposed floor drain. It was nothing if not innovative. For a guy who made it up as he went, it turned out pretty well. It was one of those add-in projects that, to the right home buyer, might look like a decent perk. But to the average plumbing code inspector, it would look more like a check box item on his running list of violations.

The new shower provided us an alternative to taking baths, and I'm no plumber, so the whole project looked good to me. It was a little weird taking a towel down to the dank basement, but given the convenience of not having to wait ten minutes for the bathtub to fill, it was a small price to pay. The shower was proof again of Tom's handiness around the house. As he was the oldest child, more often than not Mom turned to him when home projects beckoned. And while he rarely complained about the burden of duty, the fact that he did them so capably alone meant the rest of us boys were left to learn those skills on our own, later in life. On occasion, Tom did enlist us to help him on a project, but more often than not, he found it was easier to do things himself. If he was the construction foreman, we were painters.

Chapter 10 - Backyard

OUR BACKYARD WAS A SMALL rectangular patch of urban lawn. A sidewalk bisected it down the middle, providing a walkway out to the alley. The walk also divided the tree side from the non-tree side. There was a tall, hulking elm a few feet from the alley by the garage. Like all of its brethren in the front yard, it eventually fell victim to the boreal plague known as Dutch elm disease. One by one, trees were marked with a telltale red spray-painted band ringing their trunks. It was the mark of death. I remember actually shedding tears as a kid when the city crews came down our street with their saws and chippers and cut down every tree on the block. It was a tree holocaust. The street and surrounding neighborhood took on an entirely different feel—an urban forest turned urban prairie, literally overnight—almost like a tornado had come through. Our backyard tree was part of this giant slaughter just like all the rest.

Another much smaller, scrappy tree stood all gangly near the property line with our neighbors to the east. It was an ugly tri-trunked abomination that served our purpose well, an elevated home for our tree house. Tree houses were not commonplace in our neighborhood, but this particular specimen provided the perfect foundation for our childhood escape. The idea was originally hatched by Paul, who was always looking for a way to use his hands and youthful architectural savvy. Rob and I offered to help where we could. For raw materials, we scrounged up some scrap lumber we found in the junk pile next to the garage and then scavenged more from other locations. I won't say we were willing to dumpster dive for a good piece of lumber, but we were young, capable climbers and our budget was limited.

The project started with hammering four makeshift steps into the tree. This crude ladder looked like a drunken zipper running the length of the lower trunk. The steps themselves were neither OSHA certified nor guaranteed beyond about an eighty-nine-pound weight limit. Next, supporting trusses were nailed in to create a triangular shape between the three trunks. We didn't mess around with tools like levels and tape measures. We relied on cruder methods like a good old eyeballing and a few on-the-fly architectural tweaks. Appearance was important, but always took a backseat to functionality and utility. Our end goal was simple, to provide a secluded space for conducting our boy business. We might not have realized it at the time, but what we were building was our first apartment. It was going to be a rent-free, one-room bachelor pad. It didn't need to have resale value or curb appeal, and it most certainly didn't.

Once the trusses were in place, the floorboards were hammered in. A large square was left in the middle where the trap door would be positioned. A couple of old hinges were used to attach the door to the floor. This entry point was undoubtedly the coolest part of the whole tree house. It provided a single point of entry from below and kept out the girls, not that any girls were fighting to get in. But if they were, we were ready.

After the floor was finished, we set to work on building the walls. Plywood was affixed to the three trunks, forming a triangular living space. A single window was cut in one of the walls to provide a bit of light and airflow. Our roof was simply a roughhewn piece of plywood secured with a few nails, finishing off the construction quite nicely. Once the exterior of our little shack in the sky was done, it became apparent it needed some interior decoration. A little paint, shag carpeting, and a few Van Gogh prints on the walls, perhaps? As luck would have it, for our shopping convenience, the Greek church down the street had a pair of large green dumpsters that sat in their parking lot. During their spring housecleaning that year, these were filled to overflowing. Rob and Paul came across the spoils of this effort and, well, as the saying goes, one person's junk is another's treasure. Between them, they pilfered a significant number of slightly used tapered candles and about a dozen cans of dirt brown spray paint. From their perspective, both items were nearly as good as new, and that was enough to justify the dumpster diving. To them, it was a form of repurposing at the tail end of the product life cycle.

Most of the candles ended up in the attic for Tom and Pat's hangout area for their high school friends. Looking back, the fact that we had candles in our tinder-dry attic is utterly frightening, but somehow they managed not to burn the place down. After their take, a few of the leftover candles found their way into our backyard hideaway, because every good wooden tree fort needs a fiery light source, right? It's a good thing Mom never made it up the steps into our enclave. She would have fainted dead.

The salvaged brown spray paint served to give the inside of the small room a bit of darkened homey character. Well, homey for cave dwellers and bridge trolls. When we finished painting the interior walls, we discovered a secondary use for the leftover paint. We found that when dispensed in front of an ignited lighter, the paint cans made highly entertaining blowtorches. I recall sitting cross-legged with one of my brothers, holding a lighter in one hand and the paint can in the other, creating a mini flamethrower that shot a six-inch flare out the nozzle. I was transfixed. Amazed by the power and the energy, my pyromaniacal tendencies bubbled to the surface. Much of the attraction was the fact that it was completely unsafe. It rolled the elements of stolen goods, fire, and a gun together into one big offense. Of course, I was brutally aware that if Mom found out, I would be grounded for a hundred lifetimes. I was a sneaky little criminal, however, and, like the big criminals, the threat of discovery or incarceration only fueled my lawlessness.

By God's grace, nothing ever happened to any of us when we toyed with destiny using our explosive paint cans. However, the act alone was a demonstration of the freedom the tree house provided us. It was our refuge from the peering eyes of the outside world. While sometimes it led to the nefarious ways of kid-stupidity, it also served as a buffer space between youth and adulthood. When we climbed those rickety ladder stairs, nothing changed for us physically, but in our minds, we were suddenly little adults. This was our first kid pad, our independent living area away from home, both horizontally and vertically. It was where we played cards, read *Mad* magazine and *Richie Rich* comic books, and listened to Steely Dan and Led Zeppelin on the transistor radio. It was where we sugared up on Mike and Ikes, Twinkies, and Gold Medal Pop to power us through our day. But most of all, it was our haven from the rest of the world, a space in the between earth and heaven where we could goof off beyond the eyes of prying, corrective adults. It was hideous, dangerous, and best of all, completely ours.

***

OUR ONE-CAR GARAGE SAT in our backyard on the edge of our lot. It was a humble structure never intended to do much more than keep snow off a vehicle. It had a manual lift door that not only squeaked like the second coming of Godzilla, but also required Popeye forearms, steely determination, and a sailor's vocabulary. Mom regularly channeled all these elements in order to get the door open and the car parked. That garage was all we had, despite Mom often referring to it as a "knocker-downer." Although there was no love lost for the building, she did use it during the winter months. She was a big believer in getting a vehicle out of the wind, in hopes the thin wooden shell would ensure her car started on those frigid mornings. I remember her telling us the common thought of the day was wind chill factors didn't affect the starting of cars, but she wasn't buying it. She'd been through enough jump starts to know better. So, the garage it was. In Minnesota, you need every edge you can get during the brutal winter months.

Because most of the houses on our block were on small city lots, the building was stationed about five feet from our neighbor's, a two-car knocker-downer. The small dead space between the two served a couple of purposes. It was the perfect place for the burial of dead animals, either wild or, occasionally, a family pet. The space was out of sight and would better allow an animal to "return to the earth" than putting it in Mom's flower garden and risking her coming across a kitty paw or turtle shell while planting her mums. The other purpose behind this hidden space was more personal to me and my sneaky deeds.

One of our seventh grade art projects at St. Luke's was to construct something out of toothpicks and glue. We were told to bring in a box of toothpicks and a bottle of Elmer's to class and instructed to make something wonderful. Under the direction of Sister Patricia, we set about making boxes, bridges, houses, and, for those less ambitious students, an abstract pile of sticks 'n' glue. Everyone knows art is in the eye of the beholder, and toothpick artists remind us that sometimes it is in the eye of the visually-impaired creator too. I took to the tediousness of the art like a fish to water and built myself a fine-looking log cabin, complete with a realistic-looking pitched roof.

When the projects were finished and graded, we were allowed to take them home. I took a liking to the art form and started making more toothpick structures in my free time at home. I was always pretty good at meticulous building projects requiring fine motor skills. It was a meditative release for me; a chance to get some of my best thinking done. Much like my plastic modeling hobby, I became obsessed with the building process. I was the geeky kid who spent hours in his room with glue and plastic or wood, assembling awesomeness. It was kind of my thing.

Over time, I constructed an entire mini village of a few houses, a church, and a hotel. The little wooden toothpick structures began to be too much for the bookcase on which I displayed them. As I became bored with the art form, there was only one solution for the urban sprawl I had single-handedly created.

My wooden village needed a good fire.

An innate, albeit unhealthy, fascination with all things fiery always caused me to think of this solution first. Most other kids probably just threw them away. Not me. I had invested too much time in them for such a simplistic ending. So, one summer day, I picked out a couple of the houses and headed downstairs. I stopped in the kitchen and grabbed a pack of matches from the junk drawer and a few Kleenex to serve as kindling and went out the back door. I knew the perfect place for this man-made disaster would be that space between the garages. The space was exposed to our alley, but it was little traveled, so any cars that might pass wouldn't see me. All of this thinking precluded the fact that the neighborhood garages were dry, wooden tinderboxes of their own, but details like that never entered the mind of this juvenile pyromaniac. It seemed pretty harmless and not like I was doing anything wrong, anyway.

Nothing to see here. Just burning down a small village, officer.

I squatted down and stuffed the Kleenex in the underside of one of the toothpick houses. After setting it upright, I struck a match and put it to the Kleenex fuse hanging out the bottom. The Kleenex burned hot and fast. Before long, the toothpicks began to ignite and feed the blaze. The fire worked its way upward quickly and, after a few seconds, the whole structure was flaming. As the roof timbers burned, they curled at the ends and turned to ash. I imagined little people rushing out of the house as I gazed fixedly at the mini-inferno. The spectacle was mesmerizing. There was something inexplicably gratifying about watching the flames consume the toothpicks, leaving just a shell after only a minute or so. When the fiery climax was over, I stamped the ashes into the hardpan dirt with a sneakered foot, making sure there were no smoldering bits left over. Then I stuffed the larger toothpick hotel with the other Kleenex and repeated the arsonic process. The building was nearly twice the size as my first, so it burned slightly bigger, and hotter. Again, I stared at it, watching the flames lick out the windows of the structure like they would from a real building. It was pure childhood wonder in a caveman-staring-at-the-campfire sort of way.

I can't explain my fascination with fires or my need to start them. I only know that to me it seemed completely normal, like an urge any boy would have. It was almost as natural to me as reading a book or shooting buckets. It seemed a harmless form of entertainment—as long as it was contained, mind you. I had a healthy fear of any fire getting out of control. After the experience, several years prior, when I almost burned the house to the ground using my closet for kindling, I knew the power of Big Fire. Little Fire was cool. Big Fire was a bad thing, a force to be reckoned with, and potentially catastrophic. I'd run from Big Fire in the past and I didn't want to have to again. My goal was to keep the thrills small and contained.

And, this time at least, I did.

***

MY INFATUATION WITH FIRE was companion to my love of explosives. When summer rolled around and the incendiary contraband started to flow on the black market, I was a firework junkie. My purchases were usually a third-line deal; I bought them from one of my brothers who bought them from someone else. I could never afford much more than the small stuff, mostly firecrackers, ladyfingers, or bottle rockets. Every once in a while, someone would score an M80 or a silver salute, both of which were the holy grail of "holy crap!" Those could blow your hand off, or at least distance you from a digit or two. When you lit those things, you didn't linger, you *made tracks*. Their explosiveness rattled windows in the neighborhood. Furthermore, you never knew when you would come upon a rapid-burning fuse. Everyone hated those. With normal fireworks, you typically had three full seconds to throw and run. These fast burners were some sort of bad Chinese practical joke that cut the explosive time short when they hit some sort of unexpected hyper-burn. They left the igniter checking his hand after chucking the thing. At a minimum, they got your attention. In hindsight, a flak jacket, goggles, and ear protection would have been more pertinent fashion than the cutoffs and T-shirt that I tended to live in all summer long.

My brothers Tom and Paul, both of whom had an even bigger obsession with fireworks, taught me all the techniques to make creative use of whatever incendiaries they might have obtained through their network. Tom trained me up in the glories of shooting bottle rockets out an upstairs bedroom window from a Tab pop bottle. You had to be careful not to hold the bottle too near the neck or risk burns from the sparks shooting out the bottom at launch time. The nice thing about holding the bottle was the directional control you had, as opposed to just setting it on the ground. Light the fuse, point the bottle, turn your head slightly, and pffffffttttttt, pop! It was such a simple pleasure, though I am certain our neighbors hated us. I know I would.

It was Paul who taught me the art of making the mother of all rockets; the orange juice can, lower-orbit space shuttle. The construction materials consisted of an empty four-ounce orange juice concentrate can and an old tuna can. We carried the materials out to the alley and cut a small hole, just big enough to hold a single firecracker, into the bottom end of the orange juice container. Then, a little water was put into the tuna launch pad. This supposedly served to form a seal around the bottom of the rocket, but mostly it just looked cool.

Next, the juice rocket was set in the tuna can and the fuse was lit. We all took a few steps backward and braced ourselves for launch. The firecracker went off with a bang and the can shot twenty feet in the air. We squinted into the sky, watching to see which way our canned rocket would drift in the winds of the day. Then we went racing to see who could catch the can on its reentry. Because everyone knows the only thing more thrilling than shooting a can into the sky is catching its smoking shell afterward.

The alley served as our own little Cape Canaveral, and this was our Apollo moment. Statutorily we were breaking the law. Class C exploding fireworks were forbidden within Saint Paul's city limits at the time. One might say there were ordinances against ordnances. That didn't deter us, though. We were just a bunch of bored kids using firepower to kill time, manufacture a thrill, and shoot a juice can skyward. It was the kind of activity I wouldn't want to catch my own kids doing, but if I did, I could certainly relate. Heck, I might even want to light one myself.

Chapter 11 - Pets

WE HAD A NUMBER OF DOMESTIC pets during our years on Portland. Unfortunately, most of our tales are love stories turned tragic. Family meets stray cat. Family loves stray cat. Stray cat realizes the implications of a six-child family. Stray cat hits the streets, never to be seen again. These short-term relationships were the product of how my family rolled in the '70s. Between us kids, someone was continually bringing in a transient cat or "free" dog from a friend. We always loved these pets, but, because of their typically short stays, our attachments grew more superficial as they came and went. There was no sense in getting too emotionally involved with an adopted tomcat or mutt. Most tended to be runners and drifters—hobo pets, if you will. Over time, we realized they were likely only passing through with a short stint at our house on their way to another home or, worse, an untimely death.

While we had many forgettable pets, there were a few that stand out as memorable for various reasons. Fat Cat is one of these. For some reason, he never got a real name. Whether this was because our family was lazy or lacking in creativity, I'm not certain. It was most likely his assigned name because he never earned anything more dignified. He was an overweight gray tabby, big at the shoulders with an ample feline rear end. His distended stomach sack flapped from side to side when he walked or trotted, almost dragging on the ground at times. Though he was a short-haired cat, his coat was constantly in shed mode, involuntarily expelling itself from his oversized frame.

He was one of a number of stray animals that had the misfortune of choosing us as their adopted family. These animals typically did this after warming our hearts to their unique quirks and loveable characteristics. With most of them, we eventually unearthed the character flaw that pointed to the reason they were a stray in the first place. Street fighters, runners, chewers, barkers, and sprayers—we found them all. It makes sense when you think about it. After all, people who truly love their pets rarely let them run wild through the neighborhood. It was usually the ones with a penchant for shredding furniture or trashcan diving that got shown the door by their owners in hopes they'd never return.

Fat Cat was one of these unlucky strays who happened upon 1121 Portland. His pleasant disposition and fat cuddlability made him irresistible to us kids. We'd seen him about the neighborhood, and one day, my brother lured him onto the porch and, eventually, into the house, using a piece of bologna or a hot dog. Like the old adage, "If you feed a stray, they'll never leave," Fat Cat held up his end of the deal.

Over the couple of years we had him, our family didn't do much to help him with his weight problem. Like most of our cats, we tried to feed him cheap dry cat food. But, in typical cat-snob form, he would have nothing of it. He turned up his nose at the offer and went on a short-term personal hunger strike. He seemed to quickly forget that in his not-too-recent past, he was homeless, hungry, and on the street. In actuality, it was partially our fault for enticing him into our house using bologna in the first place. If we had tried to coax him to us with dry food, he would probably have continued on down the block looking for something better. And, so, the more expensive wet cat food it was.

At this time in the '70s, when Fat Cat was at the pinnacle of his girthful glory, electric can openers were all the rage. Ours was a Swing-A-Way model that sat on our counter next to the sink. When we used it to open the canned food, he came lumbering in at the closest thing to a run he was capable of. Any time we couldn't find him, we just ran the can opener for a few seconds to lure him out. His superpower was eating, so he had ultrasonic hearing when it came to the beautiful song of the Swing-A-Way.

Like most of our cats, he was allowed to roam free in the neighborhood whenever he wanted. Usually, after dinner, he just stood by the door and meowed, and one of us six kids would let him out to hang with his cat gang, or whatever it was he did. Try as we might to domesticate him, he wanted nothing of it. He was a hobo cat, made for the road. I don't know if it was more acceptable back then to let your pets roam, or if, as a family, we were just oblivious to how wrong it was. I would certainly never let my two cats run free like that today.

To add another variable into his love for the road, our house was situated near a very busy parkway. One early fall day when I was a teen, I came across a dead cat at the junction of this parkway and our alley. The cat had been there a while and had suffered blows from the tires of many passing motorists. It looked more like a cat Frisbee—flat as a Wham-O. Oddly enough, it had the same gray color as Fat Cat, who'd been missing from the house for about three weeks.

Hmmm, I wondered. *What are the chances . . . ?*

I decided to bring my brother Rob down to the death scene to help with the carcass identification. He walked up to the deflated, cardboard-thin feline, took one look, and said, "Yep, that looks like Fat Cat."

I tried to lighten the mood by saying, "Well, I guess we should call him Flat Cat now, eh?"

Rob cracked up as he reiterated the cat's new moniker. "Flat Cat. Good one!"

We agreed we should probably give him a decent burial, or at least get him out of the roadway. So, we headed back home, got a snow shovel, and scraped him onto it, with care, like an oversized animal spatula. Then we carried him home, undignified, in a kind of two-man dead-cat parade. We grabbed a spade from the garage and dug a shallow hole in the hard ground next to the garage. A shallow grave was all he needed given his current state of flatness. We slid his now svelte body into the ground like a cat pizza and covered him up. While no prayers were said, we both admitted we would miss having the big guy around the house.

***

SAM WAS ANOTHER SHORT-HAIRED gray stray that somehow found our house and its promise as a place of rest, a clean litter box, and a stinky dish of Little Friskies. I'm not sure how he got his name, but one thing was sure, Sam had a thing for late nights and the ladies. He headed out "tomming" right after dinner most weeknights, slightly later on the weekends, of course. The next morning, he showed up at the door around 7:00 a.m. drunk with love or, more often, bearing the battle wounds of his latest scrap. Tufts of hair were sometimes missing and occasionally he was sporting an open wound. Other times it was an eye swollen half-shut, suffered at the paws of a swifter tom, or perhaps a tangle with a coon or mutt. Yes, sir, Sam was a player and a fighter, all right.

There were a couple of trips to the vet when his wounds warranted medical care. The vet offered advice about keeping him indoors, but it never worked, in large part because of Sam's persistence. In other instances, he used his quick reflexes to escape by bolting for an open door when we least expected it. He was a fighter with street smarts and mad skills.

As he got older, Sam took up the nasty habit of "spraying" around the house. This behavior is often linked to territory-marking and, in some cases, can signify a urinary tract infection. One thing is for sure, the smell can knock you over. It is an odor that is a mix of ammonia and skunk. My wife and I call it "spunk," and it is nearly impossible to get out of whatever it is on. Clothes, furniture, bedding, nothing is exempt. The best way to deal with it is by burning the item and burying the ashes good and deep. Sometimes cats can be broken of this bad habit. Sam was different, though. All attempts to quell his foul tendencies were for naught. Finally, Mom had enough, so the decision was made to give him up for adoption at the Humane Society.

On the day of reckoning, Mom and I corralled Sam and put him in the carrier. He growled his guttural best for the entire two-mile trip. When we got there, I grabbed the carrier and walked in with Mom. We approached the attendant at the counter and introduced ourselves and explained our situation. After filling out all the paperwork and paying a surrender fee, the man opened the carrier and tried to wrest the cat from it. Sam was visibly agitated by the sights and smells of the unfamiliar surroundings. Barking dogs and no doubt a sense of his fate made him restless and anxious. Despite all this, the gentleman was able to get Sam onto the counter. When the attendant was briefly distracted, Sam was able to get free from his clutches. He jumped from the counter and bolted for the door, which had just been opened by an incoming pet owner. Sam shot out the door with the attendant, Mom, and me all in hot pursuit.

By the time we got out, Sam had climbed a tree in the woods behind the building. The attendant went back in and brought out another employee to help him. The two of them tried coaxing the frightened cat out of the tree with no effectiveness. We hung around momentarily, not sure quite what to do. When we were assured the situation was soundly under the control of professionals, Mom and I left and headed home. It was clear Sam was born to run and, as it turns out, born to climb, and wasn't going to go down easy. To this day, we are not sure of his ultimate fate.

***

TONTO SHOWED UP ON OUR DOORSTEP one day, and after a courtesy feeding or two, decided we were okay. Before we knew it, he had become a part of our family. Unlike many of the other strays, he lived with us for a long time, well into his teens. He was a large, good-looking gray cat with the healthy coat of a Chartreux or maybe a Russian Blue. Like Sam and Fat Cat before him, Tonto rounded out this period of family history where, for whatever reason, gray cats were our thing. No one seems to recall why Tonto was assigned the name of the Native American, politically incorrect sidekick to the Lone Ranger. It didn't really fit his nature as a big old tomcat, but the silliness of the name sort of grew on us over time. After a couple years of calling him Tonto, we couldn't really picture him with anything different. His name was nothing, if not unique.

Like Sam, Tonto had a thing for the lady cats to go along with his reputation as a capable fighter. One could surmise that he used his skills in one as a pathway to the other. During his peak tomming years, there were several instances where we let him out at night and didn't see him for several days. On a couple of occasions, we even put his food dish away, thinking he was gone forever. Then, one day, he'd show up unannounced at the back door, meowing and looking up at us like we were stupid. He looked at us as if to say, "What are you looking at, buddy? Are you gonna let me in or not?" Like most of our cats, he made sure to cash in on all of his nine lives.

After one particularly brutal encounter, Tonto came home with a nasty gash on his side. It was apparent he had been on the losing side of a fight. A large patch of fur was missing and the wound looked sore and was pus-covered. Mom guessed he might have been in a scrap with a raccoon or maybe a faster, stronger cat. She decided he should be checked out, so my brother Rob and I were tasked with taking him to the veterinarian. Mom's car was being used by someone else in the family so we were left with only my brother Tom's truck. Tom had no interest in cat dealings, so with a bit of reluctance and a cautionary lecture he gave his blessing to use his new Chevy Light Utility Vehicle (LUV) pickup for the job. It was a good-looking small truck with a fire-engine-red paint job and a white topper over the bed. Tom loved his new vehicle; it was his pride and joy. As an eager, newly licensed driver, Rob said he wanted to take advantage of the offer and drive to the vet. I conceded to his enthusiasm, but wanting to drive the new truck myself, I said, "Fine, but I get to drive it on the way back."

It was a battle of wills to corral the cat. Rob and I chased Tonto from room to room, trying to capture him. After a ten-minute pursuit, we eventually cornered him. For reasons unknown, we did not own a pet carrier at the time. Using our best teenage innovation, we used a cardboard box covered by a towel. It was an animal carrier abomination, to be sure, but it was all we had to work with. Rob and I figured it would work out just fine. After all, we were the pet owners, and our freshly captured ailing cat would surely submit willingly to his captivity and pending medical treatment.

I was charged with cat duty and took my place in the front passenger seat, boxed cat in my lap, while Rob slid behind the wheel of the truck. Because these were the days before seatbelts were mandatory, neither of us buckled up. The vet was a short three-mile trip, so it seemed like no big deal. What could possibly go wrong? As we puttered past the first few houses, Tonto, sensing some inherent weaknesses in his makeshift cat jail, began to work his way out. His sharp claws poked through the towel and scratched at my hand. I tried to stretch the towel tighter with little success. It seemed like every time I got a paw pushed back in, another one appeared from a different gap. It was like a twisted version of Whack-a-Mole, Punch-a-Paw. During our sparring match, it became clear that Tonto and his claws had the upper hand in this fight.

As the truck moved up the block, gaining speed, Tonto became more and more agitated. He started to work his head and upper torso through the gap between the towel and the side of the box. My efforts were in vain, as he swiftly maneuvered out and onto my chest. At the end of the block, Rob took a right turn and started giggling at the antics of the cat and my attempts to pry his claws off me and stuff him back in the box. He slipped and slithered through my hands onto Rob's arm and shoulder with his claws fully deployed. Rob's attention turned exclusively to the free-roaming frantic cat. He swatted at Tonto and inadvertently began to accelerate as the truck slowly drifted to the right. In the midst of the chaos, I looked up to see us heading toward a parked car.

"Look out!" I screamed.

Wham!

Our truck slammed into the car with such force it was pushed into a third vehicle parked in front of it. Rob and I executed our best crash-test dummy impersonations and, at its apex, my head hit the windshield with a thump. I saw stars as we crunched, recoiled, and spun out into the middle of the intersection. The engine revved and howled, screaming a racket like spoons in a garbage disposal. When we stopped moving, I shook my head and looked over at Rob. He was knocked out cold and bleeding from the lip after apparently hitting the steering wheel.

After I regained my wits, I tried shaking Rob into consciousness. "Rob. Rob, are you all right?" I reached over to the steering column and shut off the howling engine.

A few seconds later he slowly opened his eyes and came to. He looked at me, blinked in confusion, and, upon realizing what had happened, muttered, "Ooohhh, Tom's going to kill me."

The first thing I could think of to say at the time was, "It's okay. I'll go get him. You stay here." In hindsight, I realized that was equivalent to me saying, "Let me go get him so he can kill you."

I opened the door and Tonto scrambled out of the cab with catlike indifference to the carnage he just wrought. I staggered into the street and down the block toward home. I kept thinking, wow, are we going to be in trouble when Tom hears this. At our house, I walked in the door and saw Tom sitting on the sofa. "What are you doing home already?" he asked.

"We got in an accident!"

"An accident? Where?" Tom asked, wide-eyed.

"At the end of the block."

"Are you guys okay?" Tom asked, seemingly more concerned about us than his new truck.

"Yeah, I just bumped my head. Rob was knocked out, but he's conscious now."

We ran up the block to the scene to find him standing outside the truck, bleeding from his lip. Tom checked with him to see if he was all right.

"Yeah, I'm okay. I am sooooo sorry about your truck, Tom."

Tom reassured him it was all right and told him not to worry about it, despite his shock at how badly the truck was damaged. The force of the impact pushed the radiator fan against the grille so the fan would no longer spin even if the truck was in running condition. The right front fender and hood were badly crumpled. Indeed, after we had finished with it, there wasn't much to love about this LUV.

Fortunately, neither Rob nor I were badly hurt in the crash. Tom and Mom both had good insurance, and after a few long weeks, the truck was restored to near-new condition. Tom was forced to live without it during the peak weeks of hunting season, a fact he reminded us of repeatedly over the years. After all, hunting was the primary reason he bought the truck in the first place. To his credit, though, I still remember his first reaction was to ask about the health and welfare of Rob and me.

Three days after the crash, as my mother was leaving for work, Tonto stood waiting at the front door. He came back home like the prodigal cat. His wound had scabbed over nicely in the time since his near-death experience. Mom let him in the door as she muttered, "Stupid cat," and continued on her way to work. Tonto went on to live as a family pet for many years thereafter. At some point in the early '80s, he contracted some sort of ear infection that caused his ears to lop. Another more deliberate trip to the vet assured us there was nothing that could be done, so for his remaining years he looked a little ridiculous. We still loved him, but it was more difficult to look at him without smiling and feeling pity on the poor beast.

Some might look at our series of transient cat fosterings of long ago as neglectful. I prefer to look at it as giving a second chance to cats whose fate was day-to-day anyway. We did the best we could, given the nomadic nature of these animals. We showed them love and affection, gave them food and shelter, and yet, sometimes they still chose life on the road or even in the trees. They each played a role in shaping our family, some as foster cats, others as long-time residents. One thing is sure, Tonto certainly left his mark on our family folklore.

And all it took was a little LUV.

***

LANCE WAS A CHEWER. He was also a German shepherd whose energy and nomadic instincts eventually led to his demise. But mostly, he was a chewer. He was a big, healthy one-year-old dog with a brown coat that tapered into black, covering his midsection like a saddle. He had thick, coarse hair, a lumbering gait, and clumsy paws. His size and energy were necessary traits to fend for himself in our family. His black-muzzled face and spunky character made him irresistible when we met him at the Humane Society. We knew he was at the shelter for a reason, but with lots of kids around to train and correct him, we figured he could be reformed and made into a great dog. Like many of our pets, we rescued him from a fate slightly worse than life with us.

Early into his new start on life in our home, his character flaws surfaced and soon enough it became clear that correction of these was unlikely. It simply wasn't happening. He had his bad habits, and we would have to deal with them. What we neglected to take into account was his size. Bigger dogs are capable of bigger damage, they can run faster, and their strength makes them difficult to handle. Lance had all three of these qualities and, looking back, it is brutally apparent that his vices were probably what landed him in the shelter in the first place.

He had large dog teeth and used them for amusement as well as grinding his food. One of his favorite pastimes was chewing shoes. Dress shoes or sneakers, it didn't matter to Lance, he liked them all. In our big family, someone always needed new shoes, so when the lifespan of a pair was shortened because of a stupid dog, well, it didn't sit well with Mom. And although shoes were his favorite, nothing was off limits to Lance's destructive ways. When the shoes were put away or hidden, he took out his hostilities on the legs of furniture. One day, Mom came home to find the leg of a stuffed chair chewed like a rawhide bone. She always took great pride in our house, so this kind of thing drove her crazy. The incident was almost Lance's last dance. Fortunately, he was loved by all of us kids, so we pleaded our case and Mom let him stay.

Shortly after the chair leg, though, there were a few other events where Lance's chewing habit almost led to a trip back to whence he came. Like the time we came home from school to see he had chewed all of our Halloween pumpkins. We walked into the living room and found a jack-o'-lantern bloodbath. Bits of pumpkin face and scalp littered the living room floor at the scene of the crime, while the perpetrator sat there grinning with pumpkin on his breath. Or the time he got onto the kitchen counter and managed to reach a bunch of bananas, which he chewed and partially devoured. Still another time he got a hold of a bag of potato chips and proceeded to drag them around the house; a sprinkle here, a sprinkle there. It was clear he had a diverse palate, if nothing else.

But all of these pale in comparison to the time he knocked over a paint can and tracked it through the living room carpet and up the stairs. Mom's jaw dropped when she saw the tracks. "That rotten dog! All over my carpet! He is destroying this house," she exclaimed and put her face in her hands. After a lot of soap, stain remover, and elbow grease, we were able to lift the paint out of the carpet and restore it to its nearly original state.

***

LANCE WAS STILL A PUPPY when we adopted him, which meant he had almost boundless energy. On occasion, my brother, Tom, chose to tap into this energy and use it for what he saw as good purpose. Well, good by older brother standards, anyways.

Tom regularly assigned us younger siblings various chores on an ad-hoc basis. Sometimes they were specific, laid out earlier in the day by our mother before she headed off to work. Things like weeding the garden, cleaning our rooms, or shoveling the front walk. Other times, he made up tasks either to fit his agenda or just to remind us who was king. I was a pretty obedient kid. At eight years old, I usually did what I was told. Occasionally, though, I bucked authority. It was my way of testing the boundaries as an answer to what I saw as an unfair monarchy. Like the serfs of the Middle Ages, I never won, but that didn't stop me from raising a revolutionary skirmish every now and again.

I don't recall which command I chose to defy that sparked my unusual punishment one cold winter morning during Christmas break while Mom was at work. It was probably something significant on the order of not doing the dishes or failing to fetch Tom a glass of milk. As I said, I don't remember, but my recall on the subsequent disciplinary action, however, is crystal clear.

"All right, you didn't do what I asked you, so now you're going to get it," Tom said.

"Oh no, I'm scared!" I said with sarcastic scorn.

"Put on your boots, go outside, and run a lap around the house."

"In my pajamas?" I asked.

"Yes. And to make it interesting, I'm going to give you to a count of three and then let Lance chase you," Tom said

As bad as this might sound as a punishment, part of the kid spirit in me thought it might be kind of fun and maybe even give me a good laugh. I put my boots on and the three of us went out the front door and down the steps into the cold winter daylight. Tom said, with a wry grin on his face, "You ready?"

"Yeah, I guess."

"One, two, three, go!" he shouted.

I took off like a winter Olympian, determined to get a fast start and minimize the dog nips to my thighs and butt. After a five-step head start, Tom released Lance, who took off like a greyhound chasing the rabbit. As I headed toward the first corner of the house the frigid, cold air became secondary to thoughts of the lunatic dog behind me giving chase. I quickly understood how gazelles accelerate from zero to sixty miles per hour when pursued by cheetahs. The adrenaline took over and I let my flight response take its natural course. I high-stepped through the snow at top speed, like a skinny, Caucasian Billy "White Shoes" Johnson. I gasped and huffed as my clodhopper boots with the Wonder Bread bag liners nearly came off in the deeper drifts. My saving grace was that Lance had to negotiate through the same snow I did. As much as my two legs struggled, Lance had four working against him. Nevertheless, I was breaking trail for him and giving him an edge I didn't have. Along about the time when I thought he'd caught up, I'd gain a step or two on him, the sidewalk providing me traction while his long nails slipped and skidded.

Understand that Lance was a gentle dog who wouldn't intentionally hurt anyone. But he was capable of tackling kids and gently teething on them. Like a bear pursuit, your best defense was to curl up in a ball, take the beating for a bit, and hope he'd lose interest. Having been a victim of his playful aggression in the past, I was determined to win this circular hundred-yard dash in order to avoid becoming his human chew toy again.

I heard his huffing, snorts, and labored breathing behind me as I slogged around the house. Never more than a few steps ahead, I kept focused and ran the best pajama sprint of my life. As I rounded the last turn, I realized I was going to make it unscathed. I sprinted up the steps to the front door, where Tom was watching as an unofficial judge to this redneck Olympiad. He was greatly amused. As I put my hands to my knees and tried to catch my breath, he let Lance back inside the house with a little verbal praise. "Good boy, Lance. Good boy."

After he was done praising Lance, he looked at me with a grin and said, "Cold, Jim? You should really get dressed." He reared back and laughed heartily, amused at his own joke. When it was over and done with, I realized that while I may have lost the battle with Tom, I served my penance, and decided to take winning the race against Lance as my own little personal victory.

***

IN ADDITION TO HIS UNLIMITED energy, Lance had a heart full of wanderlust. The combination of these two ingredients was a recipe for disaster. He frequently bolted out the front door, inadvertently left open for a moment too long, and took off at full lope. Typically, the person responsible for the escape went screaming after him in chase, knowing they would likely spend the next half hour running through neighbors' yards calling his name. "Lance! Come back, Lance! Lance!" We called his name repeatedly in hopes the correct combination of neurons might sequentially fire in his wee dog-brain and remind him it was *him* we were calling.

To his credit, there were moments of lucid cognition when, upon our approach, he would stop for a moment and actually look like he remembered we were his providers. Then, as quickly as that happened, the Frankenstein half of his brain kicked in and he galloped away. Eventually, after three or four of these cat-and-mouse exchanges, he lost interest in the chase game, or perhaps just tired out, and surrendered.

One of Lance's finer escapes took place when I was out walking him one summer day. I was eight years old at the time and skinny as a poet on welfare. Lance didn't outweigh me, but in the weight-to-muscle quotient, he had the advantage, straight up. I leashed him and started down the block, trying my best to play the role of master. But from the outset, it appeared Lance was clearly in control. He tugged me along, yanking my arm in and out of its socket as he sniffed and explored. I walked along behind him and tried to keep pace. Before long, he spotted another dog halfway across the parkway and took off running, hauling me in his wake like a human drag chute. It was a bit like dog sledding—without the sled, or the snow. To an observer, it was probably pretty clear who the alpha male was—it was the furry one on the dumb end of the leash.

I did my best to try to rein him in but in the process started giggling, partly at his raw strength and partly at the developing nature of my situation. Like many boys of that age, I wasn't paying attention to what mattered, and, while looking down at the ground, I was led leash-first into a streetlight. I dropped Lance's leash as my body shuddered like a slammed door. He sped across the parkway while I rubbed my head, gathered my wits, and started out after him. With the aid of some neighbors a block away, we eventually corralled him. I started off toward home and gave him a real tongue-lashing along the way. "You were a bad, bad dog! Naughty dog! Bad Lance!" There was no show of remorse from his smiling German shepherd muzzle. He had moved on from this event to wondering what was for dinner.

Lance's love for life on the run and the great outdoors eventually got the best of him. He slipped out of the house one day when one of us kids was talking to a friend through an open door. He took off with a sense of purpose, almost like fleeing the nest for the last time. We put a chase on, but he won that time. His date with destiny was not to be denied. We looked for him for hours, but never saw a trace. He was last seen heading southeast down Lexington Parkway.

Sometimes I wonder what adventures Lance came across during his vagabond days after he ran away. Perhaps he came to his senses, was found, and turned into a service dog for the blind, or even the police force. He might have pulled little Billy out of the raging Mississippi River and run barking for help. Or maybe he just ran to a bigger house with better food. It's not that he wasn't loved as a pet; it just seemed he was like the rebellious teenager determined to do it his way. I don't know where he ended up, but all of these possibilities still cause me to look twice whenever I see someone with a German shepherd and think to myself, Lance?

***

OUR EXPERIENCE WITH LANCE kind of traumatized us as to the rigors and responsibilities of dog ownership, to the point of waiting a couple of years before we got another dog. Pumpkin, a black cockapoo male, was that dog and ultimately turned out to be the most cherished pet we ever owned. He had curly black fur, sad brown eyes, and a sweet disposition. He was great with kids and snuggled with anyone who had time. Never much of a barker, he was the consummate good dog. He always wore that happy, stupid dog grin that has a way of captivating your heart.

His only downside was, well, his backside. Because his fur was so thick and curly, he had a tendency to get dingle berries back there. Unfortunately, dogs are neither trained on how to use toilet paper nor have the dexterity to carry the process out if they were, so they are not to blame for this unpleasant affliction. My siblings and I were purposed with clipping away these rump clumps on a regular basis. It was a job we all hated, including the dog. Had Pumpkin not been so loveable, we likely would have balked even more.

On one of the long summer days when we were all off from school, I took Pumpkin out for a walk. He was a very obedient, easygoing dog, so oftentimes I walked him without a leash. It was never a problem, so I set out that day with Pumpkin to stretch his legs and let him wet a few trees. It was only to be a trip around the block, so wouldn't take more than twenty minutes. As we neared home, we walked along busy Lexington Parkway. It was at this point he spotted my sister Jane across the road. She saw Pumpkin and realized he was starting out toward her. She shouted, "No, no, Pumpkin!" Of course, all he heard was her calling his name, and he dashed headlong into traffic to try to get to her.

At the same moment, a car cruising at the thirty-mile-per-hour speed limit crossed paths with the dog. The driver hit the brakes, but it was too late. Pumpkin got rolled up underneath the car and wailed that unmistakable whine of an animal in agony. It was like the repeated high-pitched scream from the shower scene in *Psycho*, except in dog voice. My heart dropped in my chest and began racing as I realized what had happened. My worst nightmare had been lived out. My dog—our dog, had been hit. The driver put her flashers on and pulled over. Jane and I both raced to Pumpkin to find him conscious, but unable to move his back legs. Jane started to cry as she knelt down to pet the injured dog. The distraught woman who hit him apologized profusely. "I'm so sorry. I didn't see him until it was too late."

Jane gently scooped the dog into her arms. His breathing was labored and he was no longer reacting to our voices. Within a few minutes of being hit, he shut his eyes and died in Jane's arms. I began to cry, knowing it was my fault. Had I known he would do something so spontaneous and reactive, I would have leashed him tightly and it never would have happened. We took Pumpkin home and then to the Humane Society for burial. It was a sad, sad day in our family. My mother still looks back wistfully and says, "Pumpkin was such a sweet dog." There is no more fitting description than that.

***

THERE WERE A COUPLE OTHER dogs as well as a number of smaller, less domesticated creatures that served as pets in our house over the years as well. Paul had a recessive Doolittle gene and seemed to be the source of most of them. He gave turtles a try for a while. They were kept in a small bowl with a ramp, a little water, and a single plastic palm tree. As I recall, one of them escaped the small turtle paradise and was never found. Another just died spontaneously in its shell. I wouldn't rule out bored to death as a probable cause at all.

Paul also kept a garter snake as a pet for a time. Mom forbade snakes in the house, so it was relegated to the garage. It lived in a small fish tank with some greenery and a few sticks. In true snake fashion, it managed to somehow squeeze its way out and escape one night, never to be found. It was a good thing Paul wasn't in charge of housing anacondas or lions.

Muffy was a white mouse Paul bought from a nearby pet store. I'm not a big rodent fan, but Muffy was almost kind of cute. Unlike a turtle or a snake, mice have a soft coat and a degree of charm about them; at least the clean domesticated ones you get at the pet store do. One thing the pet store owner forgot to mention was that Muffy was pregnant. Within a couple of weeks, we suddenly had about seven mice on our hands. This extended mouse family was cause for the charm to wear off in a hurry. At Mom's encouragement, Paul farmed the baby Muffys out to friends until he was back down to just Muffy.

And, finally, there were a few birds as pets over the years, too. Birds, we discovered, have a high mess-to-cuddlability quotient. They kick seed everywhere and their cages needed cleaning entirely too frequently. Couple that with the fact you can't really snuggle with a bird in your lap while watching television, and I never saw the great attraction of the finches and parakeets we kept captive. Granted, there were a few lively moments when one escaped its cage during cleaning that were at least mildly entertaining. But given the choice between a pet that loves you and one that kicks its food around and craps on its floor, well, I'll take the former anytime.

Chapter 12 - Church

IT WAS IMPORTANT TO MOM we all be educated within the parochial school system. With the exceptions of a short stint in public grade schools when we were living in the housing projects and later, when Rob and Paul went to public high schools, we all came up through the Catholic school system. Our grade schools were St. Agnes and St. Luke's and both were staffed with the requisite nun population to keep things disciplined and upward looking. The nun instructors were complemented by a blend of both men and women lay teachers. As part of our curriculum, our classes always included Religion, which probably served to ground us in our faith more so than attending church. We never attended Mass much more than sporadically as a family, with the exception of the obligatory Christmas and Easter services. Most Sundays it took more than Mom had left in her tank to try to drag six unholy kids out of bed and make them holier within the walls of St. Luke's Church.

St. Luke's was a massive poured concrete structure that hulked at the intersection of Lexington and Summit, literally across the street from our house. With its slate roof, faded green gutters, and high vaulted ceilings stretching heavenward, it represented both the largesse and wealth of the Catholic Church. It was almost like a little piece of Saint Peter's Square right across the street. The main sanctuary was breathtaking. Dimly lit with large chandeliers down the length of the long aisle leading to the altar, it commanded reverence from everyone entering. As students, we were taught to be quiet and respectful during church. The echoes of voices off the polished marble floor and cavernous walls made keeping this rule difficult. If Sister Patricia didn't hear your hushed talking directly and admonish you with a furrowed brow, certainly God caught the echo from the floor and made note of it in his tally book of venial sins. I'm convinced a couple of my fellow classmates are still praying off the penalty for slamming the kneelers down loudly enough to turn heads and crane the necks of fellow worshippers. When they dropped they sounded like a court gavel from the bench of God. It was a squirrelly middle schooler's way of being legitimately disruptive and irreverent in the name of maybe getting a laugh.

The right side of the main aisle was lined with a couple of closet-sized confessionals. Once or twice a year during school hours, students were required to attend confession in the suffering confines of these de-sinning chambers. For myself, those sessions were comprised of dreaming up the correct sin counts in the hopes of trying not to appear too good or too awful. Would the confession of fighting with my sisters three or four times be enough, or too much? How about lying to my mom twice? Enough, or not enough? I also have to ask, is it wrong to lie while confessing one's sin? I think probably, yes. At a minimum, it has all the trappings of a vicious cycle.

While sin numbers were all important through my eyes, in effect, I had darker sins than those I dreamed up in the pew waiting line—the sins of my thought life. These were the ones every boy has, but dares not confess at the risk of shocking the priest and causing all kinds of unwarranted alarm. Somehow, wanting to kiss the back of Meg's neck and run my fingers through her beautiful long hair during seventh grade math class didn't strike me as something our priest would think was normal sinful behavior for a thirteen-year-old. So, instead, I stuck with the safe sins of fighting with siblings and lying to my mother.

I remember entering the confessional once, kneeling down before the screen of shielded anonymity, and starting in on my laundry list of fabricated missteps, blunders, and wrongdoings. I was well into item number two before I heard the secondary screen slide to the left. "Shhh, I'll be with you in a minute," the priest said through the dark screen. Evidently, he was still listening to another student's sins on the other side of the confessional. It seemed in my eagerness to get my walk-in absolution over with, I had trodden on the airing of iniquities by a fellow sinner. I wondered if that too was a sin; the selfishness of thinking myself so important without waiting for clearance from God's mediator. Or maybe I was just overthinking the whole thing. In any case, when he finally got back to me, it required a transgressional restart and recount. I struggled to recall whether it was three or four times I fought with my sisters.

I was eternally grateful when, in eighth grade, thanks to Vatican II, we were allowed to give face-to-face confessions to a priest in a small, more inviting chapel. It was amazing how bringing confession literally "out of the closet" helped me be more honest about my errancies. Putting a face to the person on the other end brought forth truth and humility not found in the dark, muted confines of the confessional. Being able to look God's agent in the eye, in some cases even evoking a smile, gave a comfort level to the experience not found in the format carried forward from the previous century. I know some devout, old-school Catholics had issues with some of the progressive changes brought about by Vatican II, but with regards to this method of confession, I only saw the good. In my case, taking away the screen between me and the priest took away a level of disconnection with God as well. It turned fear and anonymity into truth and transparency.

***

WHILE THE MAIN SANCTUARY of St. Luke's was very traditional, suited for the splendor of high Masses filled with incense, organ music, and the holy-yoga trifecta of sit, stand, and kneel, the basement of the church was entirely different. Its services were more contemporary and geared to the younger crowd. To me, it seemed a refreshing change to the Sunday Mass experience. To a Catholic raised in the traditional church, the format probably seemed bohemian or even sacrilegious. Instead of the large booming pipe organ music played upstairs, the basement service music was driven by stringed instruments like a guitar, and a stand-up bass. Once a month or so, the big draw was the melodious blend of voices put forth by the Williams couple. An interracial marriage, these two brought such complementary vocal styles to the sanctuary a person could not deny that God was real, he had an ear for talent, and had gifted these two with generous amounts. Mrs. Williams had a vocal range on the order of Grace Slick and Janis Joplin all mashed together. Her husband sang in baritone accompaniment a half-beat behind her in synchronic perfection. I realized how wrong it was to go to a worship primarily for the music, but when it was rumored the Williamses were scheduled to sing on Sunday, it took away the thought of sleeping in. We were never regular attendees, but Mom took notice when the Williamses were on the program.

I all but abandoned my Catholic allegiances long ago, but I did not lose my faith. Largely through the discipleship of my good friend Pat, my beliefs are stronger than ever. He mentored me through my college years and helped me establish a Biblical understanding of the Gospel I might not have attained on my own. Over the years, I have built on this through various churches and people I feel God has placed in my life. At the same time, I attribute this continuing dependence on God, His grace in Jesus, and the promise of the hereafter in large part to the foundation laid down during my years in the Catholic school system. It set the wheels of faith in motion.

To that point, I had a situation a few years back where my aunt Helen died after a long battle with failing health. My mom, still a practicing Catholic, offered to help serve communion for the service and was in need of another person to administer the wine. Because she knows I'm still a church-going Christian, she asked if I would assist her. When I said I technically couldn't be considered a Catholic anymore and might be breaking some longstanding rule of the church, she simply replied, "Well, you're more Catholic than anyone else I can think of, so just help me out." It was like an on-the-spot mini Vatican III declaration, presided over by St. Mary.

And I'm thinking Jesus will cut us a break on that one.

***

THE GROUNDS SURROUNDING St. Luke's consisted of large swaths of striped blacktop. The bulk of it was the gigantic parking area directly across the street from our house. It served as a playground during the school year, when parking was prohibited to allow the throngs of students from the grade school to takeover for fifteen-minute recesses and an hour lunch. Along the west side of this lot was a retaining wall, atop which sat a chain-link fence to offset the residences from the hellions in blue uniforms. The south side was bordered by a two-foot-high wall of its own, built with concrete blocks that supported a small green space between the church and the parking lot.

Once my friend Pat Spahn challenged me to jump from this two-foot wall on my bike. He had done it a few times and it looked not only easy, but kind of fun. I should have taken this as a sign to decline the challenge. Pat was a bike wizard, whether he was on his Schwinn modified Stingray with a banana seat or his full-sized single speed with twenty-six-inch tires. On either, he could pull a wheelie and hold it for half a block. Jumps like these were nothing for him. He had enough upper body strength to pull the front tire up and land with both tires on the ground. His skills dwarfed my own and to me, he was a kid version of Evel Knievel.

Nonetheless, I was always up for a challenge, and after all, the vertical drop of the wall, while significant, was considerably smaller than the one I'd challenged my brother Rob to years earlier. I figured I'd learned a few things from Rob's brush with death, so how hard could it be? I knew I wasn't capable of a landing that looked as elegant as Pat's, but was hoping I wouldn't embarrass myself too bad. As Pat looked on, I took a running start on my Schwinn from the grassy area and prayed a brief prayer to Saint Christopher, the patron saint of safe travels.

I was soon to discover that Saint Christopher doesn't cover bike travel.

It appeared whatever physical requirements were necessary to keep your tires parallel to the ground during a jump, required upper body strength I did not have. When I reached the jump-off point, I pulled with mighty force, but my tires chose to follow the laws of gravity instead. I knew when my chain crank hit the edge of the wall with a grinding "skrunk" that the graceful and elegant liftoff I aspired to would not happen that day. I spun headlong and somersaulted toward the parking lot. My bike followed behind, hurling insults about my lack of technique. Thankfully I had the wherewithal to put my arms out and break my fall a bit. I don't recall much about the moment of impact other than the ouchy part. My thorax took the brunt as it crushed into my handlebars on its way to a rendezvous with the pavement. Somehow, in the midst of all of it, I managed to tuck my head to avoid fracturing my skull. After landing, I lay there writhing for a moment, taking inventory of my limbs and appendages and gasping for breath. Pat rushed over and with a look of grave, albeit smirking concern said, "Are you okay?"

I slowly got to my feet, coughed and replied, "Um, no. But yeah, I guess."

Pat chuckled a little and said, "Man, that looked tough! Are you sure you're all right?"

"Yeah. I'll be fine. I think I'm going to go home though."

I picked up my bike, and Pat and I rode back to my house. We parted ways and I went inside to lick my wounds. I'd been humiliated in front of my best friend and, evidently, all I had learned from Rob's failed jump years before was that history sometimes repeats itself. These sorts of mindless flirts with death and dismemberment were teachable moments for us, but sometimes it took a couple for the lessons to sink in. I sometimes wonder if the fact that my risks were taken on holy ground was the lifesaver for me, be it guardian angels or the grace of God.

Then again, maybe Saint Christopher was listening after all.

***

THE BASEBALL DIAMOND ON THE playground at St. Luke's was nothing more than white bases, base lines, and a pitching rubber painted on blacktop. It was a low-budget, low-maintenance field of dreams for the likes of Paul Molitor, the famous Milwaukee Brewer, Hall of Famer, and Twins coach who grew up less than a block away. But for the rest of us, the playground was mostly a field of screams. When school let out for recess, many of us boys gathered together and picked teams for touch football. We used someone's Nerf ball or, in some cases, even a tennis ball, which made the passing game a much more focused affair. During the winter months when there was enough snowpack on the parking lot, we played "Kill the man with the ball," mostly because "gently tackle the gentleman in possession of the ball" doesn't have quite the same ring to it.

But on those long summer days of July when school was out, all it took was a couple of us to wander to our friends' houses with gloves and bats in hand to drum up enough kids for a pickup game of baseball. Before long, there were seven or eight kids and we crossed Lexington Parkway and picked teams. Due to the limitations imposed by the lack of supporting players, rules were often radically modified to enable us to imagine we were playing something closer to the game of eighteen players. Some of these rule changes included:

-No hitting to right field – if you did, it was an automatic out.

-No hitting to center field – same deal.

-Supply your own catcher.

-No bunting.

-Supply your own pitcher.

-Pitcher's hand – pitcher's mound served as first base and the pitcher as first baseman.

-No stealing.

-No leading off.

-Four fouls and you're out.

-Ghost runners.

It was more of a game of what you couldn't do, than what you could. Frankly, it was difficult to keep straight all the rules and limitations set forth from game to game. Every swing of the bat required both fielders and batters to second-guess the potential outcome of the play. If there was any doubt, there were always three or four opposing rule-cops waiting to correct you if you mistakenly assumed your hit fell between the confining parameters of legality. What our opponents lacked in physical skills, they made up for in their knowledge of Umpiric Law. It's a wonder *anyone* ever scored a run.

Because we longed to be as close to the big leaguers as we could, we often used a real baseball instead of a softball. We even called them "leagues." They added an element of danger to the game. Leagues were hard, and when they were hit hard they took on an intimidating intensity. They were subject to wild bounces and hops on the sandy, sometimes uneven surface of the playground. Because these hits were coming off an asphalt surface, the ball did not decelerate like it does on grass. In fact, they seemed to pick up speed with every bounce as they skipped along the hot tar. Depending on the speed off the bat, they were sometimes fielded with a slight turn of the cheek. Poor technique for sure, one that separated us from the Paul Molitors of the world, but we were fairly sure it would feel better getting one in the cheek than in the mouth. Not that that's ever happened to me, of course. Never.

The other drawback of playing sandlot baseball with a real baseball was the sketchy mitts we used to stop the screaming line drives coming off the end of the bat. These gloves were usually hand-me-downs or garage sale purchases that were well beyond their protective lifespan. Used correctly, they served their purpose well. You snared the ball high and deep in the webbing of the glove, and tossed the batter out—or, more often, wildly overthrew first base. But, if you misplayed the ball and caught the blistering liner in the palm of the glove, well, look out. That was the area where only a thin, worn layer of leather was between your hand and the cowhide missile. When they hit, they brought to life nerve endings you never knew you had. When it happened, and it's happened to every kid who has ever played baseball, the immediate reaction was to discard the glove, grab the reddened, throbbing hand, and proceed to hop about from one foot to the other making sucking and blowing noises for ten seconds. This was followed by lots of hand flapping in an effort to reestablish blood flow to the fingers and palm. It was a self-healing ritual we took great pleasure in watching because all of us had done the same routine before. It was all part of the game. Shake it off, do the chicken dance, then rub some dirt in it and get back out there.

There were other drawbacks to playing a game intended for grass and dirt on an unforgiving surface of asphalt, sand, cigarette butts, and the occasional shards of broken glass. One particularly memorable event took place as we played a friendly game with Pat Ryan and some other friends one summer day. Pat was much older than most of us, so offered to be all-time pitcher. The game had its usual moments of disputed fair balls and stunning displays of prowess and deft athletic talent. Late in the game, my team had started to rally and I was on second base as my brother Rob awaited the pitch from Pat. A runner on second base is known to be in "scoring position," and I was determined to test the claim using my swiftness and total disregard for risk. I was playing for keeps, going for broke.

Rob swung and laid down a slow roller to the gap between second and short. I took off running in my cutoffs, a T-shirt, and my blue-bumper tennis shoes. The center fielder scooped up the grounder and threw a dart to Pat, near the pitching mound, as I rounded third running with an adolescent mix of purpose and recklessness. With the ball in his glove, Pat turned toward home and took off running. It was going to be a close play at the plate, for sure. I saw him out of the corner of my eye and the attendant adrenaline burst pushed me to run even harder. Pat reached out and tagged me just before we both simultaneously crossed the plate.

The problem arose when he stepped on my foot just as it hit the ground. Unable to pull my leg free to complete what should have been my next step, my body flung forward into one of the less elegant unintentional head-first slides I've ever executed. I instinctively thrust my arms out to cushion what was shaping up to be an impromptu meeting of my knees and the terra firma of St. Luke's parking lot. At impact, my palms and knees read the stipple aggregate of the asphalt like a Braille novel. The sand and gravel behind home plate buffed the heels of my hands with the efficiency of an industrial-sized belt sander. It embedded itself in my palms and knees, serving as a sort of home plate red badge of courage – a little takeaway souvenir to bring home with me. It was a scene of violence, carnage, and defeat. To make matters worse, I was out. Not even a run to show for the whole debacle.

After a bit of introspective writhing and lacerative assessment, I picked myself up and brushed off the portion of the parking lot embedded in my hands and knees. Pat, having survived the encounter unscathed, came over and asked, "Are you okay?"

Now, it is a well-known human instinct to take a certain amount of sadistic pleasure in another person's pratfall. It just is. We all do it. Of course we show concern too, lest we be deemed cruel or insensitive. But those displays of concern usually come accompanied with the shades of an undeniable grin from the corners of our mouths and a stifled laugh in the backs of our throats when we ask, "Are you okay?"

That was the level of Pat's empathetic concern.

"Um, yeah, ow . . . son of a . . . yeah. I'm okay," I said.

"I stepped on your foot when I was trying to tag ya. Sorry about that," Pat said with a smirk widening around the edges.

"Was I safe?" I asked in hopes of getting a sympathetic call reversal.

"Uh, no, you were out, sorry to say."

"Yeah, that's kinda what I thought."

The sting of my palms exceeded my disappointment at being called out. It hurt too much to sweat the outcome. At this point my

Jim Landwehr

"agony of defeat" sports moment seemed like a good place to wrap things up and call it a game, at least from my perspective. Adding me to the physically unable to perform list would mean a number of resulting position reassignments and subsequent rule changes. It would call for things like a pitcherless game, forcing you to throw the ball up yourself and hit, to left field only, etc. This reshuffling would make continuing the game more work than it was worth. Instead, we gathered up our bats, balls, and gloves and walked home.

My *Field of Dreams* was not cut into the cornfields of Iowa, like in the movie, but rather it was driven into the scraped palms and skinned knees of my youth. The field was part of me and I was now part of it, in a very literal sense. This was one game of many spent hitting and throwing baseballs with shredded seams and sometimes sketchy degrees of roundness between the lines of St. Luke's. Our games were simple, unstructured, and wildly fun affairs. They made the long days of summer a little shorter, and set the course for a lifetime of picking ourselves up after the collision of racing for home.

Chapter 13 - School

BECAUSE ST. LUKE'S PAROCHIAL SCHOOL was literally across the street from where we lived after the move, it made sense to transfer to it instead of St. Agnes. So, I started my fourth grade year there—never an easy transition for a kid. I was shy and introverted anyway and being the new kid in class didn't make things any easier. Most of my days were spent trying to blend in and not get called on. Because of this, I unintentionally became every teacher's model student. Not academically, mind you, but behaviorally. I shut up, kept my head down, and did my work. I was an academic wallflower.

My shyness carried over into my social life as well, especially with girls. I internalized and stuffed my mad crushes on several of them through the lower grades and middle school. Girls with names like, Lori Luedtke, Donna Deutsch, and Meg Madden to name a few. Years later, my wife pointed out my affinity for alliterative names, a strange fixation I never realized until she mentioned it. There must have been something about the sing-songiness of their names that triggered puppy love in me. Of course, I never had the courage to follow through pursuing any of these romantic leanings. I was left to hope the girls I liked would figure it out on their own, take charge of the situation, and ask me to go steady. I've heard it happens all the time.

St. Luke's grade school did a decent job at trying to socialize us as little adults. One of their events was an eighth grade sock hop day.

129

Kids were encouraged to dress in clothes of the '50s. Boys greased their hair and rolled up their jeans, and girls wore skirts, bobby socks, and saddle shoes. We had no Bryll Cream at home at the time, so I used a little Crisco from the can. A little dab'll do ya. (This formula may explain my early onset male pattern baldness, but I digress.) The day culminated with a big dance in the auditorium. The girls danced, mostly with other girls, or hung together like bees in a hive across from the boys on the other side of the room. The boys clustered like pack dogs, drank punch, and ate snacks. While I loved music and would have welcomed the chance to cut it up a bit with a girl, any girl really, I was much too shy. Instead, I hung out by the record player and acted cool with my shortening-greased hair.

Another of the social outings at St. Luke's was an eighth grade trip to the local roller rink. The whole class piled into school buses and rode out to Saints West Roller Rink in West Saint Paul. When I walked in, the thumping rock music and tapestry of colored lights ricocheting off the spinning disco ball pummeled my senses. The smell of sweaty rental skates, popcorn, and Charlie perfume lent the place an aroma of teen spirit, of approaching adulthood.

As essentially a roller skating liability, I laced up my skates and spent the first few songs circling the rink perimeter with a couple of close friends. We skated along awkwardly to the beat of groups like the Bay City Rollers and Grand Funk Railroad. I tried to make my technique look polished and natural. It probably looked more along the lines of *supernatural*. Like a boy possessed, my arms flailed as if pulled by some sadistic puppeteer. While trying to look like Joe Cool, I looked more like a spastic Joe Cocker.

Eventually, the time came along that I both dreaded and looked forward to, the snowball skate. The DJ's voice boomed over the microphone, "Okay, ladies and gentlemen, iiiiiittttt's snowball time! Boys line up on the near side of the rink and girls on the far side. This is a ladies' choice snowball. Ladies, go find your man and skate him away!"

My dread stemmed from a handful of fears. What if I wasn't chosen? What if I was left standing all alone when the girl supply ran out? That would certainly be awkward. Or, maybe worse, what if the dorky loner girl chose me? Then my dorky loner self would be forever ridiculed by my dorky loner chums back in the school hallways. A fate worse than death!

Of course, the safer route would be to sit on the sidelines like a social give-up while all the bolder kids paired up and play lovers for a song. But that would be its own form of torture. By being in the game, there was an outside chance you might actually get picked by the girl you were crushing on. I'm convinced snowball skates were invented to level the playing field; a sort of forced blind date, a human grab bag for the affectionately desperate, or an arranged four-minute marriage. You might not come out with a beauty queen, but, hey, you got to skate with a real, live girl and hardly even had to work for it. To me, this was a no-brainer.

I stood there in my favorite pair of brown bell bottoms and collared knit shirt and watched as pair after pair skated off together, each couple reducing my odds of being chosen. It was similar to standing in a lineup waiting to be picked for sports teams during recess or gym. The fast, strong, athletic kids were always chosen first. The scenario at the rink was almost worse, though, driven by outward attractiveness and popularity.

Never a fan of romantic songs back then, I can't recall what the song was but it was likely along the lines of Barry Manilow's "Mandy" or some other soul-crushing ballad. Early in the song, Meg, my personal, albeit non-mutual crush, crossed the expansive roller rink divide. She glided across with elegance and grace, her long legs made to look even longer by the two-inch lift of her skates. My heart started beating wildly. This was it, my chance for romance! I stood there all jittery when, as quickly as she came, she skated past with indifference and asked the hand of a boy farther down the line. I was overcome by an odd combination of defeat and relief. It took the edge off all the worry of having to skate with the only girl who mattered to me, but it also hurt to be so patently and intentionally overlooked.

As she skated away, my sights turned back to the other side of the rink to see who remained. The pool of girls was dwindling, but big enough that the odds of me getting asked continued to be in my favor. Before long, Jean came skating over. She was cute in a girl-next-door kind of way. Average height with dark blonde hair, she was much more my match in the looks department than was Meg, my skate partner passover of a minute ago.

"Skate with me?" Jean asked, extending her hand.

I felt the warm rush of blood to my face as I took her soft hand and replied, "Sure thing."

This moment I first held hands with a girl is one I'll never forget. Her hand was soft, her fingers slender but firm. As we started out on our first lap, I worried about holding too tight or too loose. Too tight and she might think me a masher, too loose and she'd judge me as a wimp. And then there was the whole sweaty palm thing. *Lord, please don't let that happen.*

Jean was clearly the better skater of the two of us. She assumed the lead on the rolling dance floor. If I drifted too far, she gave gradual corrections, too fast and she slowed me down. I attempted to quell my free-arm windmilling so as to not look like a complete geek. "I really like this song," she said.

"Yeah, me too," I lied. We made small talk over the music a couple of times to cover the awkwardness of this short-lived first date. My heart thrummed as I grooved to the music. It was a long, romantic song, so I knew it would be an exercise in balance, skill, and feigned coolness. To get all three into synchronicity at such a young age was no easy feat.

And then, halfway through our second lap, it happened. I set down my wheels at an awkward angle and, unannounced, I pulled free of her hand and crashed to the hardwood floor in a heap of knees, elbows, and disgrace. Other couples rerouted around my wreckage with an occasional rubbernecker gawking mercilessly at my crumpled carcass. I lay there looking like so much roller rink roadkill. For a brief moment, I considered what life in the priesthood would be like. I was surely better suited there among those committed to a life of celibacy than ever trying to win a woman's heart. That much seemed very clear.

Jean stopped and spun around to wait while I collected my limbs and swept up the shards of my dignity and shattered masculinity. She giggled a little as I quickly picked myself up and pretended to make it look like it never happened. I skated over to her, grasped her hand, and said, "Sorry about that."

"It's okay. It happens," she said, smiling as we resumed our slightly more tenuous courtship. This whole girl thing was harder than it looked. As we got back into rhythm and skated around the oval, I hoped for a little grace from my partner. She seemed pretty cool about it, albeit embarrassed it happened in plain sight of all of her girlfriends.

Inexplicably, a couple of laps later, I fell a second time. Once again, I parted the Red Sea of happy couples skating near us. I looked up at Jean, who had a shocked expression on her face. Her empathy could no longer penetrate through the embarrassment and humiliation she was suffering at my sweaty hand. As much as I tried to laugh it off, it was a bit like the Olympic figure skater who falls a second time during their program. The crowd continues to root for them fully realizing their hopes and dreams are dashed. This was my Olympic moment and judging from the look on Jean's face, this relationship had a lifespan that would end at the last note of the same song it started with. A girl can only take so much.

I stood up, took her hand one last time, and we resumed our first, and what I deemed likely our last, skate date. We plodded forward around the large oval until the song mercifully ended. She turned to me and thanked me, and I did the same. I skated over to the lounge area to sit and channel my inner Charlie Brown. My first real encounter with a girl had gone as badly as anyone could have feared. For a shy kid like me, it was a real blow to my ego. I sat and smoldered for a few minutes, feeling sorry for myself.

About that time, the DJ started up Bachman Turner Overdrive's "You Ain't Seen Nothing Yet." He cranked it up a notch so the opening guitar riffs were jangly and captivating. It shook me out of my funk and back to life. I loved the song and couldn't resist. I walked clumsily on the carpeted floors over to the rink. I shook off my moroseness and joined my friends in this arena of adolescent joy. Love would have its day another time.

***

SAINT LUKE'S SCHOOL HAD a couple of opportunities for students to engage in volunteer service. One way was to serve as an altar boy for the Sunday Mass. The other was to serve your time on the police patrol where kids were issued bright orange stop flags to assist students crossing the streets of the neighborhood. This is a position that has since been replaced by adult crossing guards. Apparently, putting children into the middle of a dangerous traffic stream wasn't a good enough idea to stand the test of time. While service as an altar boy didn't much appeal to me, after hearing all of the good things about the year-end police patrol picnic hosted at Como Park, I decided I wanted to be part of the force. I was never quick to step into unfamiliar realms, so this was a stretch for me. My one-year tenure on the force ended up revealing I was probably a better fit for a career in black than in blue.

The duties of a police patrol-person entailed manning your assigned corner for half an hour both before school and after. Then, when one or more children wanted to cross the street, you put yourself in harm's way, flag first, in order to stop traffic from running them down. Despite my desire to be assigned the busy parkway corner nearest my house, I was assigned a much less busy corner a block and a half away. It was quite a letdown when I heard of my placement. I'd wanted to co-patrol the corner near my house with my friend Pat as my first choice, but they were in need of volunteers on the block up the street, so I was assigned my own corner at that location.

I served my post dutifully on a daily basis. I reported on time, protected my patrons, and always took good care of my flag. The job didn't seem so bad after all. I could do this. All of that changed within the first month of my service. I started getting harassed by a couple of students. They heckled me from across the street.

"Hey, puss boy, nice flag!"

Other times, it was just a threatening gesture or a menacing glare in my direction. As time went on, they got more brazen and threatening. They disregarded my weak attempts at juvenile authority by never waiting for me to put up my flag so they could cross. After a while, this didn't actually bother me at all and I stopped putting the flag up for them. A good automotive rundown on these guys might make the world a better place, I thought. Terrible, I know, but when you're being bullied, you think these kinds of things; a sort of middle school Dirty Harry retribution. It would certainly make my life easier. It might be a slight blemish on my police record, however.

"So tell me again, Mr. Landwehr, you never flagged the oncoming car that hit these two innocent boys?"

"Nope."

"And tell me, do you feel any remorse for letting these boys get hit by the speeding vehicle?"

"Hmmmm . . . ummm . . . I guess not."

I was a police boy vigilante, ridding the world of middle school thugs.

I held these fictional court proceedings in my head quite often with regards to these two kids. It was my first and only experience with bullies. The kicker was they were a grade below me. They were "tough kids" known for getting in trouble and skating on the edge of the law. I was on the other end of the spectrum. I was a small kid, fearful and entirely nonconfrontational. My mantra was to live and let live, so when these punks singled me out for no good reason, I had a hard time understanding why. What had I ever done to them?

Over time, their tactics became all I could think about. I was always an internalizer and the anxiety these confrontations caused took over my life. I began to dread the thought of going to school.

The ultimate showdown came one day when we met in a standoff. Bobby, the main thug, stared me down with his thugly eyes and dared me to throw the first punch. There were two of them and one me. I stood there contemplating the possible outcome.

After a brief stare-down, I kept walking. Evidently the big, tough bully wasn't quite bold enough to take the first shot. It was clear he was more mouth than action. Verbal intimidation is sometimes the worst kind and it was surely working in this situation. Nonetheless, I was relieved it didn't come to blows. They say it's the quiet ones you need to be careful of and, for all I knew, I might have ended up blowing a gasket and unleashing some brutal, deep-seated beating upon the kid. Or maybe I would have gotten my butt whooped. In any case, it never happened. The incident prompted me to request a switch to the corner near my house. It turns out a spot had opened up and I was finally reassigned to the corner with Pat that I'd wanted in the first place.

Pat Spahn was one of the better friends I had through my middle school years. When our family first moved into the neighborhood, his curiosity about us led him to just sit on his bike up the block from us and gaze our way as we hung out in our front yard. At the time he seemed more of a menacing threat than a kid interested in making new friends. He wore a flat-top haircut, which led me and my brothers to refer to him as "Flathead." We took a curious stranger, put a label on him, and made him into a villain he never was. Kids have a way of doing that, judge first, trust later. Before too long, I discovered we went to the same school and he was in many of my classes. We eventually started talking in the hallway and befriended one another.

As I mentioned before, one of the reasons I looked up to Pat was because he could ride a wheelie for half a city block, on a full-size bike nonetheless. I watched him riding by with his front wheel two feet off the ground through the picture window of our living room, turning the handlebars left and right as needed to make balance adjustments. I could never pull a wheelie for more than a few feet, let alone for half a block. Another reason I held him in high esteem was his toughness. He was the antithesis of my timid nature, which played out when push came to shove one day. We had just finished our post as police boys at the corner of Lexington and Portland and were headed out of the school after putting our stop flags away. A couple of African-American kids from a different school confronted us outside the doors. One of the boys said something to Pat and, after a short exchange, Pat charged the kid and just hauled off while his friend stood there watching. After a few seconds of struggle, they fell to the ground with fists flying. I knew Pat was as scrappy as they come, so this kid would regret having picked a fight with him. At this point, I did something I have been trying to reconcile ever since.

I ran.

Like a yellow belly coward, I took off running for home. Abandoned my friend and fled. It was flight or fight and I chose flight. I am not a fighter. I have never been. I'm a pacifist. Situations like that and the bullying incident up the street are proof. If that makes me a coward, well, I guess that's that. I am not proud I ran that day, but I did. In any case, Pat confronted me the next day in school.

"Why'd you run away like a wuss yesterday?"

"I don't know. I just freaked out and started running. I didn't want to fight anyone," I replied.

He just shook his head. His personality could not comprehend the flight option in the fight-or-flight equation. It was foreign to him. As much as I could not understand his short fuse and quick descent into a fight, he couldn't comprehend ever backing down from anyone. It took some time, but eventually he got over the incident, though I think it changed our relationship in a subtle way. One thing was clear, Pat knew who not to choose as his partner in a rumble. Both incidents taught me a lot about myself and showed me some qualities that might need some help as I grew up. I am still a nonconfrontational person, but I certainly have a better appreciation for standing by a friend in a time of need.

Chapter 14 - Sports

OUR FAMILY WAS NEVER REALLY BIG into the organized sports scene. We boys were always more into the outdoor sports of fishing, hunting, and canoeing. By default, I was considered the athlete in the family. I enjoyed most every sport that required a ball, stick, or bat and always looked for a chance to play a pickup game in a driveway, front yard, or playground. My favorite of all was football. I loved watching it, playing it, and even reading about it. For me, a big part of showing my identity with the game was centered around wearing a team jersey. Having one with a number on it made me feel better, more capable, and skilled. I'll never forget the first real one I got. I was in fifth grade and the athletic director at our school was trying to sell the extra football jerseys left over from an intramural league he ran. My mom splurged the eight dollars and got me a red one with white numbers and white stripes stretching around the shoulders. It was number sixteen, which, at the time, was Norm Snead's number, a washed up backup quarterback for the Minnesota Vikings. It didn't matter to me, I worshipped him nonetheless. The fact that I had *his* number made him a hero in my mind.

How I *loved* that jersey! Because I was not yet part of an organized team, I just wore it for the sandlot games around the neighborhood. I wore it until it was threadbare and the numbers flaked off from too many trips in the dryer. I even mended it myself with needle and thread when it ripped. I knew in our family things like the jersey were a bit of a luxury item and another one might not be coming my way for a while.

The year after I got it, my obsession with the jersey, combined with my infatuation with football, led me to beg my mom to sign me up for the city-wide intramural league. I vividly remember she took me out to Hegerle's Hardware a few blocks away and plunked down the twelve dollars for my first pair of shoulder pads; because everyone knows all good sports equipment comes from the hardware store. Mom knew how much this meant to me and made it a point to see I was equipped.

The rest of my intramural uniform equipment came from the league director, Mr. Wescott. He issued a pair of football pants, pads, and jersey to each player. Helmets were distributed from the trunk of his beat-up black Chevrolet on practice days. He popped the trunk and it was a free-for-all. If you were lucky, you got the same sized helmet from practice to practice. On occasion, you'd end up with one a size too big or too small. This meant that on a bad day, you were either looking through an ear hole for half the practice, or you felt like your cranium was in a vise. It also meant you wanted to be near his car when he pulled up to the practice field. The funny thing is, you just don't see on-the-fly equipment assignments like this today. In any case, we all lived to tell about it, so no harm, no foul.

There's something about the feeling of power one gets in a football uniform. Never mind that I was small for the team I was on – a less-than-ninety-pound weakling. Even when I strapped on the helmet that was a size too big, those tight, form-fitting pants and all the other pads, I felt like Alan Page. The only piece of equipment I spurned was the athletic supporter and cup. These were encouraged, but optional, and I never saw the need. Looking back, I don't know what I was thinking. Luckily, I never took a good shot to those nether regions or I'd probably still be singing soprano. I'm sure my kids are grateful, too.

My sixth grade team was a ragtag group, the Vikings, a team of fifth and sixth graders from schools around the neighborhood. We only won a game or two all year, but, oh, the joy of playing! I was ecstatic about being part of a team and so I took the good with the bad. Though these intramural teams were just kids, a fair amount was expected of us. Most of us played offense, defense, and special teams. Because I had a gift for kicking the ball pretty well, I was appointed to both kickoff and punting duties. The experience helped me understand why kickers tend to be loners. It's a very lonely place standing back there, seven yards behind the center. At this age, kids are good at hiking the ball to the quarterback, but haven't quite mastered the long snaps back to a punter yet. Taking snaps for punts at that young age involves a skill set more befitting of a baseball catcher than a kicker.

These sketchy snaps meant a punter's first priority was to keep the ball in front of him at all times. If there were announcers at that age, most punts would be called as follows:

"Landwehr awaits the ball to punt it away. There's the snap. Oh, and it's in the dirt *again*. Landwehr gets his body in front of it. The rush is on. The ball's loose. He scoops it up. Oh, no, he's in trouble!"

It was enough to make a coach go for it on fourth and nine.

Most of my punts were noble attempts for a kid. Twenty-five-yard line-drive kicks with two-second hang-times. The only saving grace of my kicks was the equally matched ineptitude of the poor guys who had to field them. I imagine it was just as lonely for them standing twenty yards behind their line as it was for me behind mine. My situation was not as perilous, however, because if I fumbled, oh well, the other team would have gotten the ball anyway. If the poor slob receiving it fumbled, well, that was a very bad thing. Don't do that.

While I never had a punt blocked, there were a few backfield foibles I'm sure kept my coach up at night. On one occasion, there was a perfect snap that I caught, then dropped, and thanks to a lucky bounce, it bounced right back to me. I foolishly deliberated kicking the ball, but the coach screamed, "Run, Landwehr, run!" I took off running for my life and was tackled after getting enough yards for a first down. It was a comedy of errors with a happy ending. I went from goat to hero in a matter of five seconds.

Another memorable punt came during an overtime period versus our rival, the Chiefs. We were pinned on our own six yard line. It was fourth down and long. Naturally, coach chose to punt the ball away, so I was called to action. Being a key play at a critical part in the game, I was a bundle of nerves. The center snapped it to me and I managed to shank the kick off the side of my foot. The ball did not go past the original line of scrimmage. I had managed about a four-yard punt that the other team fell on. Two plays later, the Chiefs scored the winning touchdown.

Coach was furious. I remember he said, "How can you punt it thirty yards one minute and four yards the next?" During the tongue-lashing I was thinking to myself, hey, coach, you ever punted from your own end zone at age eleven? It isn't all perfect spiral, coffin-corner punts at that age, you know?

My days as an all-around player came to a quick end in eighth grade when I tried out for the St. Luke's Spartans football team. Small, but determined, I ended up a second sting defensive end. There were bigger, stronger guys who could outkick me. The seriousness of our eighth grade team made putting my kicking shoes aside an easy decision. So a bench-warming defensive end it was. We had a great coach in Wally Wescott. His approach was firm but fair, in a Mike Holmgren sort of way.

I only had a couple moments of glory in that eighth grade season, and one of those was sketchy at best. One took place in the last game of the regular season. For reasons of pity more than ability, Coach Wescott decided I would start at defensive end for that game. I had been a backup all year and the team was coming off a great season, and suddenly I was thrust into the starting spot. My first thought was, Lord, help me to not give up any game-losing plays. These are not the thoughts successful pro athletes repeat and visualize as part of their training, that much is sure.

On the upside, the assignment for defensive ends at the grade school level was pretty straightforward. We were told to "box the ends" and keep the plays from going outside. It was that simple. Every down, box the ends and force the play inside. So on the first two plays, I'm doing a great job boxing the ends for those runs right up the middle. Hey, this ain't so hard. Then they ran a sweep to my side. I stood my ground as a pair of burly blockers rolled in my direction. They had a full head of steam as they ran interference for the tailback. When we collided, they hit me so hard my mother's mother felt it. I fell in a heap as the runner ran past into our linebackers, who were providing run support.

I remember getting up as quickly as I could and spitting out dirt between my mouthguard and teeth. Despite getting my fillings rattled, I wanted to look tough like the rest of the starters. When I went back to the huddle, our stud linebacker Tim Godfrey said, "Nice play, Jimmy!"

"Huh? I got steamrolled!"

"Yeah, but you broke up the interference."

Oh, is that what I was doing? Because it felt more steamrollerish to me. In all fairness, his comment exemplified the reason he was the defensive captain. His purpose was to build up those around him using either words or his own leadership skills. But it also showed that no decent effort was overlooked on this team. His compliment actually boosted my confidence and made the hurt easier to bear. It was proof that *everyone* had a role on a team, and was a lesson I've carried with me ever since.

Close to twenty-five years later, I wrote a letter to Coach Wescott. In it I thanked him for what he'd done for me that day. Even though I played a small part in helping us to win, there was no good reason to start an undersized, inexperienced second stringer in that final game. I told him how much it meant to me even as an adult. It showed me that a coach can have integrity beyond his win/loss record. It showed me that he was paying attention in practice when I was giving my all. And it showed he knew what such a small measure can do for a kid's self-confidence and that it could last a lifetime. Frankly, I know a coach or two today who could learn a lesson or two from Coach Wescott.

The other thirty seconds of fame in my brief young football career took place a couple of weeks later in the Parochial Grade School City Championship game. Because this was the biggest game of the year, I was back in my role as a second string reserve. In an attempt to get all the players on to the field over the course of every game, Coach Wescott put the reserves on the kickoff and punt teams. I was on the kickoff team all year, so the same held true for this big game.

The championship was a close affair. Late in the third quarter we scored a touchdown to go up by seven points. On the ensuing kickoff, I ran down the field at full speed. The return man caught the kick and started up field. He avoided the first tackle and broke a second. All that was left to beat were me and another undersized second stringer chasing him from behind. I was angling toward him and it was clear if he beat me he would score.

As I pursued him, I saw one of his blockers out of the corner of my eye. The kid was coming at top speed and, based on his angle, I figured his only chance to hit me would be in the side or back. I took his block in my left side and he knocked me to the ground. I lay there helpless as the runner continued all the way to the end zone. His teammates mobbed him as I cursed under my breath about my lost opportunity to be a hero.

Unbeknownst to me, the referee had thrown a penalty flag.

A minute later the referee picked up the flag, gave the clipping signal, and said, "Personal foul, clipping, on the return team, the ball will be placed at the spot of the foul."

The celebrating quickly silenced. Players near our bench area erupted in cheers. When I trotted to the sideline, the guys were asking who got clipped. I raised my hand, and a few of them came up to me and congratulated me. "Way to go, Landwehr!" I was a hero by default. It seems sometimes you can help your team just by giving your best, playing by the rules, and waiting for your opponent to shoot themselves in the foot.

Our defense went out and kept them from scoring and we eventually went on to win the game. After shaking hands with the other team, we climbed on the yellow school bus and started chanting, "We're number one! We're number one!" It was a noisy, sweaty, raucous celebration. Some of the guys were pounding on the ceiling, others were stomping their feet. For many of us, this was the biggest achievement of our lives, and we were determined to let the world, or at least the neighborhood, know. It seems silly to look back on that as much more than it was, but it was a great feeling of accomplishment, camaraderie, and teamwork.

Personally, I am not proud to claim I helped win the game by getting blocked illegally by an opponent. But the event was evidence once again that everybody had a role on the team. And if that was to be my legacy, to be de-cleated by an unfortunate block to deny a touchdown, well so be it. It's a dirty job, but somebody has to do it.

Chapter 15 - Neighborhood

WE HAD A NUMBER OF REALLY GOOD neighbors over the many years we lived on Portland. Decent folks who looked after the house while you were on vacation, kept to themselves when you wanted them to, and lent a hand when you needed it. Mrs. Delaney was one of them. She lived right next door and was one of the nicest old ladies I've ever met. She kept to herself, but was always friendly enough if we chose to engage in a hello or how are you? Next door to her, were the Zimniewiczs, a big Catholic family like our own. Their house sat on a corner lot so they had a large front yard that made a decent football field in the summer months, except for the towering elm tree in the north end zone that I met while running a pass route once. It was an encounter of unnecessary roughness.

The Ryan family lived across the street from the Zimniewiczs and were another of the better families we had as neighbors. The Ryan boys were close in age to many of us and were good friends over the years. They had five kids and, because their house also sat on a corner lot, it, too, had a big front yard with a smaller one in back. Later, they put in a large above-ground pool that became a favorite hangout in the summer on the occasions we were invited over.

With the good comes the bad, however, and we had a couple of those neighbors too. The first of these were the Hagens, and perhaps more specifically, Mr. Hagen. As near as I can remember, his wife never much said or did anything that bothered us. That was Mr. Hagen's job and he did it well. Mr. Hagen was an older guy, probably in his sixties when we moved in next door. It seemed like his attitude was that as long as his neighbors were white, quiet, childless, and proficient landscapers, that was fine. If they were accomplished home repair contractors, well, that was even better. A single-parent family with six kids had to rank right up there as among his worst-case scenarios. We could only be outdone by the African-American family of seven who moved in across the street. That twist in the neighborhood demographic resulted in the Hagens putting their house up for sale within a matter of a few months of the new family's arrival. He was a man of just that kind of character.

On multiple occasions, he called one of us kids to his front steps or his backyard picket fence and offered to give us a quarter or fifty cents to pick up candy wrappers and bits of litter around our house. We thought it was a strange request, but being greedy kids, we often took his money and did our chore with smiles on our faces. When our mother found out about his practices, she was embarrassed and, frankly, a little ticked off at him for being such a weasel. If he had a problem with our yard, he should come and tell her directly. After that, she told us not to accept his bribes and she took care to make sure our yard was better kept.

Mr. Hagen's yard was always meticulously maintained. He had a large white picket fence around the perimeter in the back, a six-footer with the pickets spaced out enough so you could see through it. After we moved in, I'm fairly sure he would have preferred one with tightly spaced pickets, or better yet something more Berlin-like, of brick and mortar, about eleven feet tall. Like most fences for kids over the generations, his simply served as an attractant for wayward sports balls. If one went over the fence, we either snuck in to retrieve it, or left it for him to fling back to our yard when he came across it. A near tragedy occurred a few years after Mr. Hagen moved when Tom's Weimaraner dog, Baby, tried to jump over the fence and didn't quite make it. The dog's neck slid between two of the pickets and he flailed there howling until Tom wrested the poor creature from his elevated doggie stockade. It's true, Baby wasn't the sharpest canine in the neighborhood.

The essence of Mr. Hagen's personality was revealed in a letter left on our front door one day. It was addressed to my mom and was written with a condescending and contemptible tone. In a nutshell, it outlined several areas he thought were substandard around our house and yard. I don't recall all the specifics, but I do remember him mentioning how she should have the front screen door repaired as it gave an unsightly presentation to the rest of the neighborhood. It was full of other fine suggestions befitting a nosy, meddlesome old man, everything from lawn care to child behavior. My mother took the letter personally. She seethed at the accusations that were woven through it. More than the content of it, she was upset he didn't have the spine enough to tell her face to face. Instead, he left a nasty note on the door of a widow with six kids. Again, a great testament to the depth of his character.

He was also one of those neighbors like Mrs. Kravitz who would peek in your windows whenever he could. More often than not, when you looked out your window on his side of the house, you saw the curtain move quickly as he ducked behind. It happened too frequently to be just coincidence and was downright creepy. I'm sure compared to his humdrum life, whatever was going on at our house at any given time was more interesting than watching the clock.

This snooping behavior especially bothered Tom, who was in high school at the time. We were at the point in history when the hippie movement was in full swing and Tom was developing his own "question authority" sort of rebellious streak. He had enough of Mr. Hagen's nosiness over the years and decided to do something about it one summer day while Mom was at work. He found an old bed sheet and got a can of spray paint from the basement. Then he spray painted two eyeballs on the sheet and in foot-tall letters painted the words, *The whole world is watching!* This slogan was the lash-back cry of the protestors for the injustices done to them during the 1968 Democratic Convention. Hagen's snooping and meddlesome habits were injustices Tom deemed intolerable, so he took matters into his own hands. When he was done, he unfurled it out the second-story window of his bedroom, which faced Mr.

Hagen's house. He closed the window to secure the sheet and left it there for the whole afternoon.

I don't know what Mr. Hagen thought when he saw the convicting banner. Knowing him, he didn't get the joke. If he did, I imagine he was rendered speechless. I also don't know if my mother ever found out, but I suspect if she did, she probably covered her mouth with her hand to stifle the laugh and said something to the effect of "Tom, really . . ." She did that so as to not appear to be a bad parent. It was equal parts scolding and support for what she knew was a just action on the part of her kid. It was her way of saying, "Atta boy, son! But don't ever do something like this again."

To him, it was an afternoon of sweet justice, hippie style.

***

MR. HAGEN HAD SOME FANATICAL tendencies about his property, so we were pretty good about keeping off of his lawn. And while the Hagens had a nice big fence in their backyard, they didn't have one in the front. Nevertheless, he still wanted to make sure we didn't forget where his front yard ended and ours began, so he put up a temporary foot-high fence between his yard and ours. The pitiful little plastic sections were about three feet long and a foot high each, and ran the length of his yard, down the steep hill, and lined the sidewalk at the bottom of the hill. It was a pathetic attempt at staking his ground. Even as a kid, I remember thinking, what kind of person does something like that? The fence was pitiable and met its ugly fate in a cataclysmic event that took place one summer day.

On a warm, muggy day in 1972, my friend Matt and I were sitting at his house looking for a way to escape our boredom. The novelty of the first month off school had given way to manufactured fun and homegrown mischief. With Mom working her eight-to-four-thirty every day, we were left to go feral in the summer. Scheming and collaborating on harebrained ideas were a direct by-product of our boredom.

"Hey, why don't you pull me behind your bike in that wagon of yours?" I said.

"That sounds cool! Let's do it. I've got some rope in the garage," Matt replied. I followed him into his cavernous garage where he foraged among the paint cans and garden tools. After a minute, he found an eight-foot length of clothesline. "Yeah, this'll do the trick." Then he pulled the beat-up red Radio Flyer wagon out from the corner and we headed back outside.

"If we start at the top of the block, we'll have a nice downhill to build some speed," I said.

"Yep, and it will be easier to pedal, too. Good idea."

We walked the bike and wagon up the block. Next, I tied one end of the rope to Matt's seat post and the other end to the base of the wagon handle. Matt steadied his bike as I climbed into the red wagon behind it. It was a tight fit for a ten-year-old boy of my size; my knees were tucked up halfway to my chest. The handle, the only source of steerage of my homemade suicide cart, was pulled back between my knees. I was about to discover the need for steering was strictly incidental anyway when you were being pulled by an oblivious, borderline sadistic bicyclist. After all, where would you turn? What would turning bring to the table anyway? Mostly disruption and upheaval, is my guess. Our combined engineering brain trust didn't think that far ahead, though. We were more focused on an immediate summertime thrill to liven things up in the neighborhood. We ascertained that the combination of the gentle hill and Matt's pedal power would provide the appropriate g-forces to attain just that.

At this time in the '70s, there were no bike helmets. In the case of a wreck, our modus operandi was to "tuck and roll" and pray for grassy landings. These maneuvers could save your life and might come in handy given the lack of consideration to a braking mechanism on the death train I was sitting aboard. If the need should arise, we thought we could just hang our legs out of the wagon and drag them in order to slow the hurtling caboose down. It's also never good when your engineering model is loosely based on braking techniques developed by the Flintstones.

I gave Matt the thumbs-up signal indicating I was ready to go. He started pedaling down the hill as I concentrated on steering and mentally drafting up my last will and testament. We started out slowly past the Wrens' house and worked into a steady churning rhythm past the McCrakens'. The melodic thump of the sidewalk cracks reverberated through the thin metal bed of the Radio Flyer; cathump, cathump, cathump. When we passed Mrs. McGinn's house, the wagon was gaining momentum and the thumping increased in intensity.

The thrill of our speed was starting to get to me. I suddenly found myself in the middle of an undeniably dangerous, but exhilarating situation. The scene was starting to resemble a driverless wagon pulled by spooked horses in the old western movies. I was hostage to a pedaling madman and all I could do was shout, "Slow down, Matt!"

By the time we hurtled past the Gerahtys' place, the wagon handle wobbled like the steering wheel of a car in need of tire balancing. It shimmied and shuddered, left to right. We were clearly exceeding the recommended top speed for the wagon; she was starting to break up. Matt seemed determined to take it to the next level, however, and pedaled on. The O'Tooles' house was just a momentary blur out of the corner of my eye. I watched intently for the unexpected bump in the sidewalk that would throw the wagon into a state of further turmoil, or perhaps even the highly feared death roll. At the Naughtons' house, the weaving started. The wagon started a slow 'S' curve weave that steadily increased. I was suddenly at the mercy of the wagon and a few laws of physics. I could do nothing but ride it out as the wagon swayed and wobbled a drunken weave as we approached the Hagens' house.

"Slow down!" I shouted again. He finally started to slow as we approached my house. It was too late, though. The wagon careened wildly into the first section of Mr. Hagen's foot-high plastic picket fence and shattered it. Pieces of the fence scattered like shrapnel all around me as I ducked my head in the chaos. Having lost all control, I continued to mow down the subsequent sections in rapid-fire manner. Pieces were flying all around me like car parts at an Indy crash. We were absolutely destroying the ridiculous little fence and there was nothing I could do about it but duck as sections fell to the hurtling hell-wagon.

It was horrifying glee!

Eventually, Matt realized what was going on and started to brake. When the entire fence length had been destroyed, I put my feet out and dragged myself to a stop. Matt and I looked at each other in a sort of dazed shock. My Lord, what had we done? It was so tragically funny we couldn't help but start to crack up. We were laughing not only at the devastation, but the fact we had done it to possibly the worst person we could imagine, Mr. Hagen. He was the Mr. Wilson of our Dennis the Menace neighborhood. What we had done was a bit like stealing a car from the chief of police. One just doesn't get away with those things. We might as well turn ourselves in voluntarily and plead guilty on all counts.

Matt and I scrambled to try to cover our tracks by rebuilding the portions of the fence that were salvageable. We quickly saw it was an exercise in futility, as most of the sections looked as though they'd been put through a wood chipper. Within a minute or two, Mr. Hagen appeared. It is my guess he witnessed the whole incident, as any good snoop would. He had his fingers on the pulse of his house, his yard, and his neighborhood. When he approached us, he was actually calmer than I expected, given the debris field before him.

"What happened here, boys?" he asked, as if it was not brutally apparent.

Let's see. There's fencing scattered everywhere, a bike, a wagon, and a couple of middle schoolers just a few feet away. Hmmm. I don't know. What do *you* think happened?

"We're sorry, but we lost control of the wagon. It was an accident," I said in our defense.

"I see. Well, you probably shouldn't do that anymore. You boys help me pick up the pieces here and then go play somewhere else," he said.

I was stunned by his lack of rage. It was a bit unnerving. I thought for sure he was going to blow a gasket and take the matter to Mom. But he didn't. Indeed, this de-fencing event showed me that perhaps I hadn't given Mr. Hagen enough credit. Maybe he, like the Grinch, had a heart after all. It was probably two sizes too small, but it might just be there. We helped him pick up the fence pieces and reassembled the salvageable parts into a post-modern, minimalist fence. When we finished, Matt and I skulked off, feeling guilty for our sins, while Mr. Hagen took the broken fence pieces and went into his house.

I felt bad about the destruction we had wrought. But I have to admit there was a sinister side of me that thought it was a bit of sweet righteousness. While I had no intention of wrecking the dwarf fence, frankly, it felt a tiny bit good. Sometimes kids help adults see characteristics in themselves they cannot see. Maybe that was what happened to Mr. Hagen and why he reacted the way he did. The saying goes that good fences make good neighbors. I became a believer that maybe destroyed, crappy little fences make mean neighbors better neighbors.

***

PORTLAND AVENUE WOULD BE JUDGED "average" by most standards for a neighborhood street in St. Paul. It intersected Lexington Parkway, a very busy main thoroughfare, but for the most part, Portland would be considered an "off" street. There were no street parking restrictions per se, so often the street was dotted with cars people chose not to park in their garages. Most of the garages were small anyway, served by a narrow alley running down the backside of the block.

Parked cars aside, the street served as the playground for my siblings and me as well as many of the neighborhood kids. Kickball and touch football were favorites, especially in the summer, when most of the cars were taken to work leaving a bigger playing field. Hot Box, where one or more players run between two basemen in a rundown, was another popular game.

The street was also the perfect venue for our Evel Knievel act. Most boys in the neighborhood were obsessed with the wheelie. It's timeless, too. Boys are still fixated with it. I can't explain the fascination except to say it takes the boredom out of those safe two-wheeled rides. Why pedal along safely on two wheels when you can pop a wheelie and risk landing on your back and smashing your skull? Who could pass up that opportunity?

As thrilling as they could be, wheelies were not quite enough for us. If getting one wheel off the ground was good, wouldn't two be twice as fun? Double danger, double risk, double fun seemed easy enough to rationalize for our prepubescent brains. To satisfy this urge to adrenalize, we set out to break the bonds of gravity by building our own bike ramp. We had all seen enough of Evel Knievel jumping over cars and buses to know how exhilarating it looked, so we set out to experience it for ourselves.

We built the ramp using scrap wood and bricks that had accumulated in the garage. The runway itself was made of a piece of plywood that rested on a combination of boards and bricks stacked up to the desired heights. Its height varied between eight and twelve inches, often depending on how much spare wood was around. We assembled the whole thing in the middle of the street, with the understanding we would have to watch for cars turning up our block. When that happened, one of us yelled "Car!" Then, one or two of the spotters would run and grab the ramp parts and move them out of the traffic lane. If the driver was a neighbor, they would sometimes slowly drive around the obstruction so as not to force us to disassemble.

Once the ramp was set and the coast was clear, we took turns jumping from the crude Jetway. Since my bike at the time was the unwieldy gigantic Huffy, I was forced to borrow my sister Jane's pink and red Schwinn, unbeknownst to her. My bike never jumped anything bigger than a curb. Her bike, with its twenty-inch wheels, was a much smaller, nimbler, and significantly less manly craft. It didn't matter to me, as I was certain my forthcoming leap of courage and daring would offset any subsequent gender taunting. I would silence the snickers and transform from "Shevel Knievel" to "Evel Knievel" after breaking all distance records and sticking my landing.

When my turn came, I straddled my Barbie bike twenty yards away, looking to get a good running start. The assigned ramp spotter and distance judge gave the signal and I started pedaling furiously toward the ramp, looking to get my thrill on. I hit the ramp with a "ca-chunk" as the plywood rocked under the weight of bike and rider. At the end of the ramp, I stopped pedaling and pulled up the front end so as not to land on the front wheel first and risk becoming a member of the dreaded over the handlebars club.

It was a perfect execution. The bike and I achieved liftoff; we were airborne! It was my own little Wright Brothers moment. Gravity defied, cares, worries, tomorrows, and yesterdays forgotten. For the moment, all that mattered was I was flying. Flying! The flight was no longer than a second or two, but it was exhilarating. It was not just complete freedom, it was a five-mile-per-hour, full-on rush. I quickly understood how people become addicted to the adrenaline rush that comes with a mix of speed, lift, and danger. The moments between the end of ramp and the beginning of pavement were like a slow-motion dream sequence.

My hands gripped the pink handlebar grips tightly, as my eyes fixed on the pavement ahead to pilot a safe landing on the unforgiving asphalt. Then, the thrill ride was over as quickly as it started. The reluctant she-bike slammed to the roadway with crushing force. The back tire immediately went flat and the bike flopped and slogged to a flatulent stop a few yards after its maiden flight. Apparently, some load and performance specifications were exceeded and the bike had served me notice. She was done playing with boys and had put an end to the nonsense.

Paul looked at me and smirked. "Aw, Jane's not gonna be happy about that," he said, glad it wasn't him who would incur the wrath of Jane.

"Dang, it was a good jump though, wasn't it?" I replied, adrenaline still coursing through my veins.

Paul climbed astride his own bike, saying, "Yep, it sure was." He was anxious to get some more jumps in before the day was over and had little time for my gloating. I climbed off the bike and walked it up our front hill and around to the garage. In an attempt to short-circuit the inevitable verbal flogging from Jane, I set about fixing the flat. While she didn't often ride her bike, if she wanted to and it was out of commission because of one of her stupid brothers, well, Lord help him. I worked quickly, removing the wheel, then the tube, with Indy raceway pit-stop speed. After the glue and patch had set, I put the tube back onto the rim, replaced the tire, and pumped it back up. It was as good as new.

Eventually Jane found out about the bike's heroic leap and the damage incurred and repaired. While she was not happy I was abusing her bike, she took a fairly soft approach with her reprimand.

"Stay off my bike," she said with a serious tone. "You have your own bike."

"All right, sorry I used it without asking," I said, happy to have caught her in a good mood. It appeared my days as a daredevil bicyclist had ended as quickly as they began. Unless I could take to learning how to jump the Huffy, a task sorely suited for such an unwieldy bike, my jumping career was essentially over. Although I'm sure my brothers shared their bikes with me for subsequent jumps, none matched the elation of that first jump on Jane's.

The solo jump I had on the bike was a life lesson for me, in many ways. We spend much of our lives looking forward to those moments of exhilaration and freedom, those times when we are flying, or seemingly walking on air. These moments, however, come bookended on one side by periods of mundane preparation and another by deflation, recovery, and repair. Life is made up of years of speeding at the ramp and fixing the flats, sprinkled with days of flying through the air. I recognize, though, that you can't have one without the other. Ultimately, it's how we cope with and enjoy the entire process that matters.

**

SCHWINN STINGRAYS WERE all the rage during the early '70s. Their banana seats and sissy bars allowed for riders to sling back low in the seat, looking cool. The seats also had plenty of room for a friend on the back, though that was reserved for emergencies. In a pinch, though, your friends could ride on the banana seat while you stood up and pedaled. We called this giving the rider a "buck." I'm not real sure where this term was derived, but it seemed to fit. The real risk takers among us took a spot on the handlebars. It's hard to believe this was ever a thing, but it was. It might be just a tad unsafe. This maneuver could only be topped by those rides featuring both a seat rider and one on the bars. These were slow moving, wobbling affairs that involved a lot of giggling and lots of navigational advice from the passengers.

I remember when Mom bought me a Stingray. It was gold and had a matching flaked-gold pillow-tufted banana seat. It was a single speed, and with its gently arcing frame and pull-back handlebars had a cool factor by design. Mom bought a couple of them and I am sure we were the envy of the neighborhood. My suspicions were affirmed shortly after I got the bike. I was out in the front yard one warm July day. My bike was lying on the front sidewalk at the base of the hill in our front yard. I was ten and goofing around with some toys on the front lawn while Tom sat on the porch swing. Along came a couple of teenagers, one on a bike, the other walking. One of them picked my bike up, straddled it, and said, "This is my bike."

"Hey, what are you doing?" I said.

"Get off that bike or I'm calling the cops," Tom shouted from the porch.

"It's my bike," the kid replied and started pedaling furiously, as did his friend on the other bike.

I stood there in disbelief at the brazen act of theft taking place in front of my eyes. Tom ran into the house and called the police. They assured him they would keep an eye out in the area, but that bike thefts happened all the time and the bikes usually weren't recovered. After the incident, Tom gave me a lecture about locking my bike whenever and wherever I left it. A year later, my mother replaced the stolen Stingray with the much less cool three-speed Huffy. I assured her I would always lock it per Tom's suggestion, and I almost always did.

Except that one time.

I rode it down to Bober Drug one day and in my haste to get my twenty-five-cent candy bar I chose not to use my lock. It was wrapped around my seat post, like always, but knowing I would be in and out in a minute, I just parked my bike in front of the store and walked in. I approached the main register area and started perusing the candy choices. Living up to the moniker a kid in a candy store, I spent my time wondering if I wanted to splurge my entire fifty cents on candy, or spend half of it on Wacky Packages or football cards. Wacky Packages were stickers that parodied various consumer products using crazy names like Crust Toothpaste and Smith Sisters cough drops. I eventually made my choices, paid the cashier, and walked out.

I turned the corner out of the store and my heart dropped. My bike was gone! Oh my God, someone stole my bike, again! I only left it for five minutes. How could this happen? I swiveled my head back and forth, looking up and down Grand Avenue. I raced around the corner of the store to an area where I sometimes parked my bike, thinking maybe I hadn't really parked it in front. It wasn't there either, so the sweating began in earnest. What would I tell Mom? I could almost hear her response: "You had another bike stolen? What's wrong with you? That's it, no more!"

I began to rehearse all the various excuses, alibis, and lies.

"They cut the lock."

"They picked the lock."

"I was bike-jacked."

Like most lies, none of them would sound convincing enough in front of Mom. I was a terrible liar anyways. Just as I was beginning to think all hope was lost, my friend Pat Ryan appeared from around the corner, riding my bike. He was laughing and taking great satisfaction in my agitation.

"Hey, what are you doing on my bike?" I asked.

"Left it unlocked, I see? I was trying to teach you a lesson. I knew it was yours right away and figured I'd give you a good scare." Pat swung his leg over and climbed off the bike, setting it on its kickstand.

"Wow, did you ever! I was freaking out there," I said.

"Well, here ya go. But lock it up next time!"

"Got it. Yep," I replied, relieved to have my ride back.

Part of me resented Pat for giving me the scare of my young lifetime. But another part respected him for the lesson he taught me. His age difference made him like an older brother to me and things like that were lessons more typical of a big brother than a friend. It was a tough-love incident I needed at the time. Oddly enough, it built my trust in him as a friend as well.

So if you ever want to solidify a friendship with someone, steal their bike sometime.

**

A BLOCK AND A HALF FROM our house sat St. George Greek Orthodox church. The church, built out of concrete block, was rectangular and squat with a domed roof covering the altar area. Atop the dome was a large gold cross. Rectangular stained glass windows in the likenesses of Christian saints were cut at various heights into three sides of the church. These were connected to each other and to a central "trunk" window using smaller glass-block cut-outs, to form a tree pattern. Like most churches, the stained glass windows served to feed natural light into its interior spaces. Architecturally, the church was nothing special, but services were always well-attended, so I suppose it filled its function well.

Since I was raised Catholic, this place of worship was a bit of an enigma. It might as well have been a Muslim mosque for all I knew of it. I didn't realize until much later that it was actually a close offshoot to our own faith. At my young age, I was oblivious to the fact that much of the Bible was written in Greek. To me it was just another non-Catholic entity and, in a manner of speaking, their faith was Greek to me.

In all my years living so close to the church, I spent hours and hours outside on its grounds, but don't recall ever going inside it. The church parking lot and grounds were where I, my brothers, and our friends hung out. It was our refuge, our turf. It was also our portal to young adulthood. Sitting on a corner lot, the church and its grounds were out of sight of our house. When we announced that we were going to "the Greek," our mom always knew we were close by. I'm not sure if the fact it was a church lent her a false sense of security about what we were doing there, but at least she knew where to find us if needed. For us, the facility provided enough green space to play a pickup game of football and a parking lot to play baseball. Just as important, the area lent us enough privacy to conduct the illicit activities of most eleven-year-olds. Our pursuits at this place, athletic or nefarious, depended on our collective mood on any given day.

The church grounds were around the corner from the Ryans' house, our best friends from the neighborhood. On the north end, the parking lot was bordered by an alley trimmed with lilac bushes and a cyclone fence. These bushes served as a sightline buffer between the Greek and the Ryans' house. They gave the boys a bit of seclusion from their helicoptering mother, who was persnickety about where her kids were, especially around dinnertime. She called them home for meals or chores by leaning out the door and ringing a large hand bell. Clang, caclang, caclang! My family always thought it a strangely antiquated method for calling the kids in, but I'll give her this much, it was *effective*. Its range was pretty much the entire city block, and Pat and Matt dropped everything and headed toward home if they heard its call.

A four-foot-high concrete supporting wall ran along the west end of the parking lot. It was our place to hang out, eat candy, spit sunflower seeds, and drink soda. On occasion, someone produced some pyrotechnics like those magic ashen snakes that were so popular around the Fourth of July. We lit them and watched as the ashes seemed to come from underground. The wall served another purpose when all we had were harmless cap gun caps. We hammered away, popping them one at a time with a rock. After losing interest, we took to smashing a whole roll with a larger rock. Who cared about one hundred little pops when you could have one huge bang that made your ears ring? There was something inherent in our male hormones that made the appeal of smoke, fire, and explosions so dangerously attractive. Or maybe it was just me with my pyro-tendencies, I don't know. In any case, these gatherings at the "Greek Wall" were frequent and never dull.

Pat Ryan and I spent a lot of time hanging out at the wall. He was three years older than me and, as I mentioned with the bike incident, I looked up to him like a big brother. He was funny, understood me, and we became pretty good pals through his early high school years. We played sandlot football and softball together and he was a great source of support for me as I navigated the waters of a new school, church, and neighborhood. Shortly after his junior year, he began smoking Marlboro Reds. I remember the first time he pulled out a cigarette pack. I knew then and there things had changed between us. He had changed. He was growing up fast, or faster than me, and this was evidence. Smoking seemed like such an adult thing to do, and I wasn't quite done being a kid yet. Over time, the wall became his favorite place to hide out and puff away.

A part of me hated to see this change. I wanted our friendship to last forever, but Pat was brutally honest with me. He said it wasn't cool for high schoolers to be hanging out with kids in middle school. He asked me politely if I wouldn't mind making myself scarce if ever one of his high school friends showed up when we were hanging out together. I told him I would and that I understood. That's not to say it didn't sting, because it did. I took it that it was all part of growing up, but I also certainly saw where things were headed. It was the male equivalent of the "we can still be friends" talk that many breakups between boyfriend and girlfriend feature out of fear of actually severing ties for good. Sometimes it worked, but more often it meant an end had come.

We remained friends, but it wasn't the same. At sixteen, he took a job working as a busboy at the Lexington, a restaurant managed by his dad. It was at "the Lex" where he picked up his smoking habit in the first place. During his last couple years of high school, he frequently said, "Let's go to the Greek, I need a smoke." When we got to the wall, he burned through two or three Reds over the course of an hour, and we just talked. We talked about school and sports, music and his love interests. Typical teen stuff. It was this place where we established the footing of our young independence. It was our little area of escape and isolation from our families, parents, homework, and chores. There was something liberating about the grounds. It was a place where we could be all the boy our genetics had dealt us. We could spit, laugh, cuss, and work out our teenage angst.

The church had a basement stairwell that was sheltered by a large brick wall. Because the building was locked and empty most of the week, we occasionally used the stairwell as our den of childhood iniquities, which seems sinfully wrong, given that it was, after all, attached to God's house. In essence, it was our stairwell to Hell. On a couple of occasions someone pulled out a dirty picture they had ripped from a *Playboy* and shared it around the group. The rawness of the images was both shocking and alluring to our young eyes. The unbelievably endowed, heavily airbrushed women helped answer some of our anatomical questions and were simply too good not to share. We were well aware if we were caught with such illicit pictures we would be grounded for a week. Surely a week's grounding would be worth it, though. It was difficult to look away. We passed them around until one of us would get uncomfortable with what we were feeling, and they got stuffed back in the owners' pockets. These impromptu viewings, these thirty-second peep shows, came with an explicit "don't tell" policy, of course. We were sneaky, not stupid. Besides, having seen them made the show-ee as guilty as the show-er.

Another stairwell vice was faux smoking. It was our friend Matt's idea. One afternoon, he held a few cigarette-sized dried up twigs he'd fashioned from the nearby lilac bushes.

"Hey, guys, do you wanna try smoking these?"

"Uh, I dunno. Maybe. You try it first," I said.

He struck a match, lit the stick, and put it between his lips. The wood was semi-hollow, so when he drew on it the end flared up and he got a good cheekful of lilac joy. He blew it out real cool like, trying to get his best Columbo or Kojak on. A couple of more puffs and he coughed a little.

"Ooohhh, it's a little harsh at times."

Enamored by the allure of coolness that came with the promise of an uncontrolled coughing fit, I said, "Here, let me try one of those."

Matt passed me one of the sticks and continued to puff away on his own. I lit the end and took a cautious drag of my wooden 'grit. It was about as appealing as it sounds, though not as bad as I feared. It tasted like a wood fire smells. I, too, tried to look natural while smoking the unnatural. Coughing is a sign of weakness and uncool among the smoking brethren, so I stifled my fits as much as I could. Frequent, shallow, short puffs kept momentarily in the cheeks were more effective at impressing than any attempts at deep draws. We pointed with them and used hand motions à la Hollywood. Then we practiced various methods of holding our wooden cancer sticks. The between-the-fingers hold was the most popular, followed by the Bogart joint-pinch with the thumb and forefingers. After a few minutes of doing our best to act cool and stifle our coughs, the appeal of our vice wore off. We stubbed out our fire sticks and trundled up the stairway steps—out of our little Hell—and back into our smoke-free lives. As addictive as real cigarettes may be, these sticks of lilac wood were shaping up to be more like a gateway drug to smoking abstinence.

***

THE GREEK HAD A LARGE GRASSY area to the east of the church, bordered by the parking lot on one side and Lexington Parkway on the other. This green space made for an almost ideal football field. The makeshift field had a slight incline and, dimensionally, was about twenty yards wide by forty long. In later years, the groundskeeper added a few randomly placed pine trees to discourage our play. It was a nice try, but the trees simply provided another obstacle we needed to watch for when running our plays.

We played on this field often. These were games where plays were sketched out in the dirt with a finger; games that usually went on until someone got hurt or was called home for the night. Our gridiron battles tended to start with four or five players but sometimes grew to as many as nine or ten as word traveled and new kids found their way onto the field. We almost exclusively played tackle football, not touch, so we tried to make the teams balanced according to size and ability in an attempt to keep the scores close.

There is one game that stands tall over all of the other pickup games of my boyhood, one of those you never forget. In it there were five of us, two on a side with Pat Ryan filling in as all-time quarterback. There was Matt, who was not much of a runner but loved to play center and block. My brother Rob excelled at running the ball, and was tough to take down. Jimmy Z just liked playing and would do whatever he was asked. I had soft hands and fast legs and was one of Pat's favorite aerial targets.

It was warm and overcast when we started. During the course of the game, the skies became more and more foreboding. Eventually, they just opened up and it began raining hard—I mean *stupid* hard. Before we had time to react, it increased in intensity. At its zenith, it was at full roil, a deluge. We were having such fun before it started none of us saw the harm in continuing despite the worsening conditions. So we played on.

The game was a back-and-forth affair. A score on a long pass was followed up by a kickoff return for a touchdown. Everyone was in the standard uniform for neighborhood pickup games; jeans, T-shirt, and tennis shoes. Our clothes were soaked and stuck to us like wet papier-mâché. Our tennies squished and oozed with every step and functioned more like skates on the slick, saturated grass. Quick, dazzling cuts gave way to more deliberate, intentional steps—lift, plant, lift, plant—in the interest of remaining upright. It was a technique we each adopted after the first few leg-splaying attempts to run recklessly at top speed.

The rain had been coming down hard for about twenty minutes, but was still not enough of a deterrent to pull us from the fun at hand. The slippery leather ball made for frequent fumbles and dropped passes. Mud was smeared into the knees of my pant legs and my favorite jersey took on pronounced brown hues. Across the line of scrimmage, my opponents were all wearing variations of the same theme, mud and sop.

What we were doing went against every convention ever laid down by our parents. *Come in out of the rain. Don't get dirty. Don't play in the mud. Don't play so rough.* Each of us knew we would get some sort of lecture when we got home, but none of us cared. It was too late to care, and besides, you can only get so wet. The damage had been done. At the moment, we were relishing the immediacy and chaos and absolute joy of right now. Whatever the cost, it was a price for the privilege of being completely irresponsible, thoroughly reckless, and utterly free.

***

DON'T ASK ME WHY, but shortly after birth young boys have a need to shoot, explode, and kill things. When my wife and I were young parents determined to raise the perfect son, we both agreed "no guns." We quickly discovered if you deny a boy a gun, he will craft a gun out of a stick, a spatula, a broom, or any other inanimate six-inch object. The list is only limited by the boy's creativity.

One of the more creative ways my brothers and I found to quell this need for shot and fire was to build a device known as a Polish cannon. The name was never politically correct, to be sure, but what boy can resist the thought of building and shooting something with the word "cannon" in it? I knew I couldn't, so when my brother Paul proposed the idea, I was all in.

Paul oversaw the construction, and started by cutting the tops and bottoms off of five or six metal soda cans (in the days before the prevalence of aluminum cans). The exception was the lowest can, whose bottom was left intact. Then, we taped each of the cans together using masking tape. Once the cannon barrel was assembled, a small hole was punched in the bottom can. When it was finished, a tennis ball was loaded into the top of the barrel, and the cannon was tapped on the ground to move the ball to the middle of the cannon. The firepower for the device was a small amount of cigarette lighter fluid squirted into the ignition hole. Then, we picked the whole device up and gave it a good shake to distribute the fuel and transform it into a highly flammable gas.

The cannon was set upright in the middle of the Greek parking lot and a gunner was chosen and given the matches. The match was struck and set to the bottom hole, and with a woosh and pop, the tennis ball blasted up forty or fifty feet high into the summer sky. Wahoo! When it landed with a high bounce, we scattered and chased down the smoldering Dunlop. The scene was a demented blend of youthful irresponsibility, testosterone, and pyrotechnics. As tennis ball rocketologists, we were guilty of discharging harmless mortars with a target of nothing more than the blue sky and a cheap thrill. We were living it, baby!

Most launches were conducted safely and without incident. On occasion, especially with a new, untested cannon, the ball sometimes got lodged in the barrel near the top. This failed launch caused a backdraft of pressurized flame to shoot out the ignition hole and singe the hair off the fingers of the unsuspecting gunner. The poor victim hopped around howling and shaking his hand, always more shocked than hurt. It was great spectator sport for those of us not holding the match. We acknowledged it was the price they paid for being the self-important chief gunner. You had to take the good with the bad; fame sometimes, flame others.

It is probably hard to conceive, but on some occasions we were a little too liberal with the lighter fluid. This resulted in the ball returning to earth bouncing around in flames. The "spotters" would circle around the flaming orb and usually someone tried to kick it back into orbit. After the novelty of the cannon wore off, the brilliant idea was hatched to spray the lighter fluid directly on the tennis ball and ignite it. Of course, this degenerated into an impromptu game of fireball soccer. If you give a kid a can of lighter fluid, nine times out of ten he'll turn it into a dangerous sport.

It seems to me that in this day of video games and overly protective helicopter parents, places like "the Greek" where kids can gather, relate, and cause a bit of mischief and grow up, are fewer and fewer. I don't know, maybe they're replaced by shopping malls, movie theaters, and skateboard parks, and that's probably okay. To me, though, it seems like a sad substitute for the freedom granted by a place with nothing more going for it than the place itself. A place where fun wasn't given to you, but where you made it up, you invented it. I'm not advocating that smoking sticks and looking at dirty pictures has anything redeeming about it. At the same time, it sure was nice having a central place, a gathering place, where we could make our way in the world. Where we could talk through things, play with fire—both literally and metaphorically—and burn off a little excess testosterone. It makes me think of the song "The House of the Rising Sun" by the Animals.

"And it's been the ruin of many a poor boy, and God I know I'm one."

In a sense, the Greek was that house for me.

***

ON A LONG, HOT SUMMER DAY in '73 or so, I was challenged to a race by Matt Ryan who had an older, smaller bike than my big brown Huffy three-speed. We lined up at the corner of Portland and Dunlap and straddled our bikes, ready to rocket. We checked for cars in front and behind and agreed that if a car turned onto our block, we'd rerun the race.

When we deemed the street was clear, I counted down, "Three, two, one, go!"

We each jammed on the pedals and jolted our bikes headlong, wobbling and weaving for the first few feet until we regained control. Matt sped to a quick lead, having a lighter bike with smaller wheels. I pushed hard to catch him, both of us standing on the pedals to achieve the best velocity. A quarter of the way, I started to gain on him as my bigger tires and higher gearing began to pay dividends. The crank turned at dizzying speed and the wind howled in my ears as I built up momentum. It was shaping up to be a close race, and I was starting to hit my stride. I pushed even harder when the unthinkable happened.

My foot slipped off the pedal.

My crotch slammed onto the bike's crossbar with neutering force. At the same instant, my sneakered foot bent awkwardly under the pedal and the top of my shoe dragged on the pavement like some sort of unhinged bike rudder. It flapped and flailed for a few moments, taking on angles never intended, leaving bits of rubber, canvas, and ankle skin in its wake. By God's grace, I managed to hang onto the handlebars and maintain a semi-straight course. I quickly assessed what life without children would be like and tried to come to grips with how to wrest myself from my unflattering and unintentional biker's tuck. I was in a tough spot, on a bike possessed, and I needed to act with immediacy and surety. This was my Apollo 13 and I needed to think like Houston.

First and foremost, I kept steering straight. There was no sense in bringing a curb or parked car into the picture to make things more interesting. Straight was good; breathe, and steer straight. At about the three-quarter mark, I reclaimed my foot from its captive pedal and flopped it back on the topside of it, being careful not to disrupt the attention and duty of any of the other correctly functioning appendages. This allowed me to stand enough to push myself back to sitting on the seat. Once I was back in the saddle, I regained my wits and clamped down hard on the handbrakes. I don't know why I didn't do that earlier, but it was probably because I was assessing the severity of my bodily injuries and trying to avoid an unintended appointment with the pavement.

I slowed the bike to a stop as Matt continued to pedal furiously to the finish line, evidently blind to the clownish daredevil act taking place behind him. I straddled the bike's crossbar, careful not to further damage the goods that had been hammered a few short seconds ago. I stood there, wincing in pain, trying to breathe through it. It's always best if no one is around when this happens because when you're working out the issue, you don't really want to be talking to anyone. Just a man, his pain, and some newly discovered falsetto skills.

Eventually, Matt figured out I had fallen into the DNF (Did Not Finish) category and rode back to where I was recovering. "Dude, what happened?" he asked.

"What does it look like? I slipped off the pedal and crushed my nuts," I said in a loud whisper.

Matt tried to contain his laughter, but couldn't. "Man, that sucks. Does it hurt?"

"Ooooohhhh! Ummm, yeah, it does. A lot," I said, as if my condition needed clarification.

"Well, I hope you're okay. I won the race, I guess."

Matt not only won the race, but he took the gold medal for compassion, as well.

***

WINTERS WERE LONG, BRUTAL seasons in Minnesota. They began in mid-November and oftentimes lingered until April like an annoying party guest overstaying their welcome. The season affected kids and adults differently that far north. My friends and I saw it as a fun and glorious change that brought new recreational opportunities not found during the milder months. In adulthood, winter was all about snow removal, ice dams, and cars that wouldn't start. It was looked on with dread and a sense of foreboding and was, ultimately, just something else to grumble about.

Some of my favorite winter activities were ice skating and hockey. Almost every playground in the Twin Cities had a rink that was set up in December and taken down in late March. These rinks were a nicety we did not have in our immediate neighborhood, so a couple of our neighbors took it upon themselves to make their own. The Zimniewiczs on the corner constructed a decent-sized one in their backyard, but because it was a tad narrow, most games had to be played at half-ice. We took advantage of theirs when we could because it was ideal for getting out and getting some brisk, fresh night air.

The Ryans across the street one-upped this setup by having the best rink in the neighborhood. This was because of their big yard and the gaping glow of their floodlights that lit the whole rink up like an outdoor arena. The Ryan brothers used the garden hose to flood the rink every few days to give it a nice smooth surface—a kind of poor man's Zamboni. Between the brothers, they kept it shoveled during the winter months, piling the snow on the perimeter.

Most of our skates were hand-me-downs that we found while rummaging around in our attic. We came across two pairs of old brown leather skates and one pair of double-bladers designed for young, weak-ankled beginners. The double-bladers were relegated to Paul because he was the only one they fit. We were fortunate the other two pairs fit Rob and me. In this case, fit meant we only needed one crumpled up paper towel in the toe of each skate to make them work. Everyone knows how difficult it is to skate with correctly sized skates, let alone trying to do it using a set of prosthetic tissue paper toes. One thing is for certain, they served no obvious benefit from an insulation standpoint. Our toes got cold quickly despite the paper towels and our doubled-up cotton tube socks.

On the Ryans' rink, a small three-step ladder was provided for youngsters to push around for balance and help them get their feet under them while they practiced their technique. While the young kids used the ladder, the rest of us had hockey sticks that we used as much for balance as for poking the puck around. Our pickup hockey games were unorthodox affairs of two-on-two with a single universal rule: no lifting the puck. No lifters! We had all taken enough shots to the shins in winters past and, as impressive as a good shin-high wrist shot looked on the ice, no one wanted to be on the receiving end of the frozen rubber missile.

During all the flailing and thrashing about in the guise of a hockey game, we sometimes lost our balance and fell on our butts. This typically started out like an impromptu Russian dance kick, with a-one-and-a-two. It quickly devolved into the victim windmilling their hockey stick like a ninja sword on the way down. The stick became a supersonic whistling cry for help as it whirled and landed with a ca-thrack on the ice. The frozen air only served to amplify these sounds, like gunfire in the quiet night. Luckily our bodies were deeply padded by layers of clothes that took the brunt of the fall. Nonetheless, as the fallen lay on the ice writhing in pain, we offered our empathetic assistance with a gushing round of snorts and laughter. This rink was full of fun, but void of compassion. This was partly because we knew we might be next. It was only a matter of time.

One particularly cold January night, I was skating with Matt Ryan and Rob. Rob and I both wore our dull, hand-me-down skates and were slogging around the pockmarked rink on our weak ankles with our hockey sticks. The dark sky was riddled with stars. The moon was luminescent, serving as a floodlight of its own while we practiced our passing and wrist shots. Play was stopped every twenty minutes to tighten our skates, which seemed to loosen themselves by design. Our skills were bad enough when they were tight. When the laces loosened, our ankles sagged and bent outward, then inward, then back outward again as if controlled by some crackpot voodoo doll puppeteer.

After an hour and a half or so, Rob said, "My feet are cold, I'm going in."

"Okay. I'm gonna stay out for a while longer," I replied.

Rob glided over to the rink's edge and then hobbled over to the sidewalk area and changed out of his skates. When he was done, he started making a snowball and then a second. I had a pretty good idea of what he was about to do, and didn't like it one bit.

"Don't you even think of it," I shouted at him from my spot on the ice.

Rob just laughed and heaved a snowball at me. When the first hit me, he quickly bent down and threw the second. Then he made another, and another. The shots whizzed by me repeatedly as I tried to stay balanced on the ice and defend myself from the onslaught. I had all the stability of one of those blow-up clowns that you punched as a kid. After the third time I was hit, I lost my cool. "That does it, you're dead!" I shouted, as I slipped and slid in his direction like a raging hockey drunk. Rob took off running, and, once I hit the edge of the rink, I did the same. I was furiously mad and determined to catch my little brother and make him pay his dues.

At the sidewalk, every step started with the blade and ended with the ankle twist. Blade, ankle-twist, blade, ankle-twist. The steel scraped and scratched the sidewalk as I gave chase. I never thought to actually look, but it's my guess I was leaving a trail of sparks. As I hit the edge of the terrace before the street, Rob was laughing hysterically. He was unable to contain himself at the sight of me sharpening my ankles on the pavement. I suspect I looked a bit like the Scarecrow from *The Wizard of Oz* when he was taken off of his post, all rubbery-legged and unbalanced. If I were Rob, I'd be laughing too. And none of this is to say anything of the harm the chase was doing to the blades of my skates, but at the moment that was the furthest thing from my mind.

It wasn't until I was across the street that I realized the lunacy of my actions. It was just in the nick of time because my ankles had nearly detached themselves from my fibulas. In any case, it was clear I wasn't going to catch him, especially since my mom wasn't keen on running with skates on in the house. At the curb, I stopped for a moment, caught my breath, turned around, and started wobbling back to the rink. Nearly breathless, I skated back out on the cold, striated ice. After a few more minutes, I conceded that my toes were cold too, to say nothing of my ankles which were the consistency of hamburger. I now understood why hockey players kept things on the ice during their brawls. Skates are not conducive to running.

***

THERE WAS ONE PARTICULARLY snowy, difficult winter in the late 1970s where the snow on Portland Avenue became compacted and hard. Snow plowing in Minnesota was an art form and was usually pretty well executed. For some reason, this winter got away from the crews and our street suffered from plow neglect. Over time, the cold weather, the incessant snow, and the compaction by passing cars turned the street icy and slick. One evening during that winter, I looked out our picture window and saw my friend Michael actually skating up and down the street. He was striding back and forth stickhandling the puck underneath the glow of the street lights. I was simultaneously shocked and intrigued. What would possess him to go skate on the roadway in front of his house? It seemed a little bizarre, frankly, even for a Minnesotan.

Because I loved a good game of pickup hockey, I was a bit jealous of Michael's improvisation. I knew he was on the hockey team at St. Paul Academy and couldn't get enough of the sport, as this spontaneous outing was testament to. So I put on my coat, hat, and boots and went outside. As I walked to the edge of the curb, I heard the scrape of his skates on the ice-covered snowpack and the clickity-clack of his stick with the puck.

"Hey, Mike,"

"Hey, Jimmy Landwehr." He often used my full name, an endearing trait of his.

"I can't believe you're skating out here in the street."

"Well, why not? It's a little slow, but not too bad," he said.

"I guess I've just never seen anyone skating in the middle of a road before."

"There's nothing wrong with it. Why don't you get your skates on and we can pass it around a bit?"

There it was, the invitation I was waiting for. All along it wasn't that I'd gone out so much to check out his strange behavior, but rather in hopes I would be asked to play. I think Michael was glad to have someone to goof around with as well.

"Okay, I'll be right back." I spun and ran into the house to get my skates. A few minutes later, I came back outside with them and my hockey stick tucked under my arm. I sat on the front steps and laced them up good and tight. Before long, I was out on the street doing large oval loops with Michael. He'd sling me a wrist shot pass that I'd corral with my stick, putter it around a bit and sling it back to him. I had to admit, the ice was less than ideal, but it sure beat sitting indoors.

Looking back, this event was pivotal in my relationship with Michael. Shortly after he and his family moved into our neighborhood a few years earlier, we'd become friends. The two of us had a similar love for sports, were the same age, and were both shy introverts. He regularly hung out on our porch or front steps and, over time, we got to be fairly close friends. This wintry night was an otherwise ordinary weeknight made special because of our mutual love for hockey and connecting with a good friend. For some reason, the night has always kind of stuck with me as memorable.

And over those high school years, despite our racial differences, race never really came into play. When we recently reconnected after falling out of touch for thirty years, Michael revealed that, at the time, he was looking for a place to fit in in his new neighborhood. Me, well, I was just looking for a friend. It turned out to be a mutually beneficial relationship. I told him I always admired him for his athletic abilities and he said he admired me for just letting Michael be Michael. He's one of those guys you consider yourself lucky to have called a friend when you look back on your life. He'd probably say the same thing about me, and much of it can be traced back to a cold night on a frozen street in St. Paul.

***

ONE OF THE MORE APPEALING characteristics of our neighborhood was the Grand Avenue business corridor. We lived just two blocks from Grand, a street dotted with a mix of retail shops, residences, and apartment buildings. Along with my siblings and friends, I haunted these establishments with quarters and dollars earned working chores. We didn't need much more incentive to leave the house than a little pocket change and a sweet tooth. There were a few businesses that stuck out as favorites and that I recall with a certain fondness.

There was the Uptown Theater, a small local movie house where you could see a show for seventy-five cents on a Saturday afternoon. One evening, my brother Tom took me to see a long ago kid-classic, *Paddle to the Sea*. It was a heartwarming adventure about a child's handmade canoe with the phrase, "I am Paddle to the Sea. Please put me back in the water," painted on the bottom. The movie chronicled the boat's travels from the shores of Lake Superior to the Atlantic Ocean. And while the movie was enrapturing, it was the preview film that showed before it that caught my attention even more. It was a documentary about the legend of Bigfoot. It gave some background showing plaster casts and such, but then it proceeded to show the controversial Patterson video footage of the beast. As a kid, this was the coolest thing going. A seven-foot gorilla that only a couple of people have ever seen? And now they have it on film! Does it get any better than that? Years later, of course, the Patterson footage was exposed as a hoax and they still haven't proven the existence of Sasquatch. But for me, the impact of this film still has me wondering, what if?

In a moment of temporary parental insanity, my mother took all of us kids to the Uptown Theater one night see John Wayne in *True Grit*. Like all movies for me, this was pure escapism. Wayne with his horse and guns took me far from the Midwestern city life I was living. The whole family munched popcorn and watched as he and Glen Campbell fought for justice and picked off Ned Pepper, Chaney, and the rest of the cowboy villains. I will never forget the shootout in the meadow, reins in his mouth, rifle and pistol blazing. Wayne singlehandedly took out all of the roughneck cowboys. Not bad work for a "one-eyed fat man," as he was referred to by Ned Pepper.

Next door to the Uptown was perhaps our favorite haunt as kids, Bober Drug. A mom-and-pop-owned drug store, this place had nearly everything a kid would need. It was the final resting place for countless quarters of allowance money spent on Reese's Peanut Butter Cups or Hot Tamales candy. If we managed to save a little more money, we stepped up our purchases to the toy aisle. Here we splurged on paper kites whose flimsy wood sticks ultimately disappointed by snapping during a crash landing or, worse yet, during construction of the "bow" that held the paper tight to the frame. Balsa wood planes were another popular item in the toy section. Like the flimsy kites, these were prone to breakage after a few flights or sometimes even during assembly. A cracked wing or broken stabilizer was often mended using an on-the-fly customization. They never flew quite the same, so back to Bober's.

Bober's was a haven for all the good and some of the bad in our household. It was where we bought Mom her Christmas or Mother's Day gifts for many years. Thoughtful gifts like a two-pound box of after-shower powder in a canary yellow container. I am pretty sure there was still a pound and a half of that powder left when she finally threw it out years later. Bober's was also where we filled all of our prescriptions. The pharmacist behind the counter gave us our orders for the amoxicillin and other doctor prescribed items. For lesser afflictions, it was also where we got our over-the-counter items. These included Rid lice shampoo to kill those parasitic critters brought home from a grade school infestation and shared around the family. Twice.

But for all of its good, Bober's was a marketplace for some of the vices of our time too. My sister Pat sent me there on a few occasions with a note reading:

My son, Jimmy has my permission to buy a pack of Marlboro cigarettes.

Sincerely, Mrs. Landwehr

She added our phone number after her signature and sent me on my way. I was dreadfully afraid of being caught in the act of such a blatant lie, but Pat always made the deal irresistible by saying I could keep the rest of the dollar's change to use on candy for myself. After the second visit to the store in a week, the suspicious clerk called the number to verify I wasn't developing a bad habit as a twelve-year-old. Of course, Pat was there to pick up the receiver and claim my mother's identity. It was always enough validation for the clerk. She was a crafty one, my sister.

Pat wasn't the only smoker to take advantage of my services. Eve was a craggy, elderly, sweet neighbor who lived in the apartment building across the alley from our house. Somehow, I got roped into supporting her habit too. Eve was well down the road on her way to emphysema and operated in secrecy from her husband, who didn't want her smoking. She called me when he was at work and, upon my arrival, gave me strict orders to not dilly-dally on my way to and from the drug store on my clandestine delivery. I felt like I was pounding nails in her coffin. But because she paid me a full dollar for my effort, well, I couldn't save her from herself with that kind of profit margin to be had. So I pounded away.

Just across the street from Bober Drug were two businesses that symbolized the epitome of small business perfection for the Grand Avenue neighborhood. Regina's Candies was a cramped store packed with sweet goodness where kids could go and get half a dollar's worth of Michigan cherries, lemon drops, or jaw breakers. I am certain our purchases were much to the annoyance of the clerks, who preferred larger sales. They were always courteous enough, but it's hard to make a living a half buck at a time. Over time, the allegiance paid off as we became teens and bought our Valentine boxed chocolates for Mom. That and a dollar's worth of Michigan cherries, maybe, too.

Next door was the other Grand Avenue gem, the Bungalow Bakery. The warm aroma of fresh baked bread, cookies, and cakes enveloped me every time I walked into that yeast and sugar dreamland. The bakery was the source of every special occasion sheet cake Mom ever bought. There was none better. We were sure to accompany Mom whenever she made a bakery pickup because, without fail, the clerks behind the counter offered sugar cookies to every child who came in the door. It was such a treat, a simple pleasure that made it stand out as a business and kept the customers coming back. There were times we'd go in and buy a couple of cookies knowing we'd get a free one just for coming in the door.

Down the street a few doors stood the Lexington Restaurant. A large, hulking building with a black marble façade, it was one of the top three black-tie restaurants in St. Paul in its day. It was where we celebrated everything from first Holy Communions to proms and graduation dinners. Since the manager, Mr. Ryan, was Pat and Matt's dad, most of us boys ended up with jobs at the restaurant for a time during high school. One of my first jobs was as a dishwasher there during my sophomore year. I worked my way up through the ranks, spending a stint as a dishwasher, then as a salad chef and as a bus boy. The job paid well and taught me the importance of a good work ethic, but the late nights were the source of many sleepy days in high school.

The avenue was lined with shop after shop like these. Hardware stores, ice cream shops, florists, grocery stores, filling stations, restaurants, and many others. It was eclectic, vibrant, and bustling. In the street fabric of our neighborhood, Grand Avenue was just another thread, albeit a major one—a seam, one might say. But it was so much more to our household and our community at large. It was a kid's economic playground, a place to blow our cash Las Vegas–style, without the hookers and riff-raff. The street served as our bus stop, our meeting place, and our avenue to other avenues. I've been back many times and have noticed the street continues to thrive today in a trendy, urban hipster sort of way. Before I moved away, word got out that Grand Avenue was the place to be. Since then, progress has dressed Grand Avenue up in skinny jeans, thick-framed glasses, and a lumberjack beard. But underneath its cool exterior and facial hair, there lies a history of Bigfoot, sugar cookies, and ill-gotten cigarettes.

***

TUESDAY WAS SHOPPING DAY for Mom, a day she faced with dread and loathing. After a long day supervising a large staff at Ramsey Hospital's Medical Records and Research Foundation, Mom drove to the Red Owl grocery store on Grand and did the shopping for the week. I'm certain she was probably exhausted by the time she got there. To help herself cope with shopping day, she imposed a strict directive on us kids to be sure to be home around six o'clock so we could help haul groceries in from the car. If she had to make more than one trip from the car to the house with bags, we all heard about it. Usually there were at least two of us to help, so most weeks we came away unscathed.

Over time, we developed the habit of meeting her at the store to "help" her with the shopping. One or more of us walked the five blocks to Red Owl and waited outside until she got there. She always made us feel welcome, but I'm certain there was a part of her that just wanted an hour of alone time to get what she needed, do some thinking, and to isolate. We certainly fixed that. Furthermore, these meetings meant her bill jumped a bit as she caved to some of our pleadings and requests for non-essential items.

While she pushed the cart, we stood on the front rail near the wheels and served as human shopping cart hood ornaments. There was something stupidly fun about riding backward through the aisles of colorful packaging, produce, and freezer products. Every aisle had its own unique smell. The produce section smelled like a tropical forest, green and lush and fresh. Over in baking products the aromas were sweet and dry like Mom's flour cupboard. The baking aisle was a kid's culinary Garden of Eden, where all goodness originated. It was also where we badgered Mom for things like brownies, Betty Crocker cakes, canned frosting, and chocolate chips. The chocolate chips were intended for baking but were frequently pilfered as a backup supply of sweets when the candy and cookies were depleted. There were so many ways to exasperate a mother, and we seemingly tapped them all.

On these weeks where we tagged along, Mom always tasked us with picking out a couple of food choices. "Pick out three sugared cereals and two regular," she'd say. Later in the snack aisle she delegated, "Get me one pack of Twinkie or Ho Ho desserts and some Cheetos or Doritos for lunch snacks." And, finally, when we rolled around to the candy aisle, "Pick two bags of candy." This was always a difficult decision for us to agree on. A couple of household favorites were orange marshmallow circus peanuts and bite-sized Snickers bars. It's a bet that our pediatric dentist was afforded early retirement subsidized entirely by our family.

While we were tasked with choosing the unhealthy, sugar-rich foods that kids crave, Mom was busy picking out all the healthier staples; the boring food. Things like two loaves of bread, four gallons of milk, meat from the butcher, and boxed potato mixes. She kept the potato varieties diverse, including scalloped, au gratin, and everyone's favorite, Potato Buds. Only during holidays did we get real mashed potatoes, which usually led to complaints about the lumps. It wasn't until I was married that I realized potatoes were not supposed to have the uniform consistency of marshmallow fluff. Needless to say, I haven't returned to my potato flake roots.

By the time Mom was done shopping for our family of seven, her cart was full to overflowing. At the register, she regularly garnered looks of disbelief and judgmental scorn from other shoppers. These people were self-righteously blind to the locust plague six kids can wreak upon the family homestead from week to week. At any one time, we had at least two and sometimes as many as four teenagers in the house. The only surprise is that Mom didn't end up using two carts. Furthermore, she was a coupon queen and never had to resort to food stamps. She was too proud for that.

At the checkout aisle, we helped her unload the tonnage from the cart as the checker clicked away at the noisy NCR register. The bag boy worked quickly and dutifully to stay ahead of the conveyor belt clog we inevitably produced every week with our goods. When the bagging was complete, Mom took a number and we followed her to the car. She steered the big green Impala around to the loading zone and the bag boy loaded the heavy brown paper bags into the back seat. Me and any other siblings present squeezed in around them and took in the smells of new boxed goodness.

When we arrived home, Mom set to putting the groceries away. We helped in our own ways, mainly by opening the sugared cereals and digging our dirty mitts into the deep recesses of the box trying to find the almighty nineteen-cent prize. This was an unsavory practice that, even in today's world, must make every parent wince. The prize was heavily sought after by each of us, which usually meant an argument before Mom came in and set peace to everything. After it was pillaged, the box took on a new level of roundness, making it difficult to fit alongside the other flat, unaccosted boxes in the cereal cupboard.

Mother, forgive us, for we know not what we did.

The other unusual practice we developed on shopping day was to hide the two bags of candy Mom bought every week, so as to slow its decimation. Each of us had our own little nook or cranny within the kitchen or dining room where we would stash the sweets in hopes anything out of sight was also out of mind. Sometimes it was hidden in the sugar canister, other times the cupboard over the refrigerator. My personal favorite was under the tabletop brace of the dining room table.

This out-of-sight, out-of-mind mentality was completely delusional thinking. It might have made us feel better but it certainly did nothing to quell the quest for candy. In some ways, it only fueled the appetite of the lookers even more. In the end it was fruitless because if the person could not find it they would complain to Mom loudly enough that she would insist we divulge the location. In the courtroom of candy justice, Mom was the judge and jury.

As petty as it seems, shopping day was always one we all looked forward to as a family. Mother's cupboards were bare by that day and the thought that we'd have access to some of our favorite treats as well as daily staples was worth celebrating. These in-store gatherings were a chance to connect with Mom and play a minor role in the meal selection at the same time—despite our choices that would make nutritionists twitch and cry. I don't know how she put up with us hanging around on those evenings, but I'm glad she did.

***

I FOLLOWED IN THE FOOTSTEPS of my brother Tom and attended Cretin High School, the local all-male, Catholic military school a few miles from my house. In high school, I only had a few really close friends. I was liked or at least tolerated by many, but my true core of good friends consisted of my four buddies, Pat, Pete, Dave, and Dan. We were as close as friends get in high school, I suspect. Most of us were introverted, shy kids and just happy to have each other. We shared many good times as we navigated those awkward teen years.

In our senior year, we had taken a recent interest in toilet papering the houses of fellow classmates after dark. As a clique, we were considered the straights. We were not into drugs or drinking so much as juvenile mischief, like transforming a house from dull and boring into one that appeared to flow with the breeze. One night after our high school football team took another beating, we were pumped up on soda and candy and looking for a way to burn off some adolescent energy. Since we were in his neighborhood, we decided to toilet paper Stan Turner's house. We knew Stan was a good guy but we were also aware he was someone who wouldn't seek us out individually and beat us up if he discovered we had done the dirty deed. The key to most crime is to make sure the victim is of equal or lesser strength and courage than you. This holds true in the arena of two-ply bathroom misdemeanors as well.

When the football game was finished we went to the local supermarket, a large, well-lit twenty-four-hour Rainbow grocery store. As a pack of five, we headed straight for the paper product section.

"Here's what we need, right here," Pete said as he grabbed the cheapest eight-pack of toilet tissue he could find.

"Oh, that's perfect," Pat said, giggling.

"We'll get three, then," Pete added.

We all started giggling at the prospect. Eight rolls would be damaging enough for most houses. Twenty-four rolls would be enough to practically gift wrap one.

"Don't you think that's too much?" I added.

"Nah, it'll be fun. C'mon, Landwehr, lighten up. It's Friday night," Pat chided.

Not wanting to be left out of the hijinks, I relented. It didn't take much. I was drunk with giddiness at the thought of doing something so wrong, yet also so apparently harmless. I'd been a rule-following goody-goody my whole life and here was a chance to rebel a bit.

We grabbed three eight-packs and headed toward the checkout area. Because it was shortly after ten o'clock there were only a few cashiers to choose from. We sidled up to the youngest female checker, who was maybe nineteen or twenty. We figured our odds were better for getting through with so much contraband by appealing to the naiveté of someone closer to our age. You certainly couldn't slight us for thinking on our feet. Oh yes, we were a sly bunch.

When Pete put his eight-pack on the belt and nothing else, the clerk looked at him with suspicion. "Yeah, I'm not feeling so good," Pete lied as he rubbed his stomach in his attempt to look legitimate.

"Oh yeah?" the clerk said, smiling. She saw the rest of us in line behind Pete and suddenly she was an accomplice to the whole crime-in-the-making.

"Yeah, plus this stuff is such a great deal. Hard to pass up," Pete added.

"Uh-huh, I see," she replied. She couldn't contain her smile anymore.

She finished ringing the sale and Pete paid her. I followed and put my eight-pack on the belt. She looked at me and grinned a bit.

"Yeah, it's something going around, I think. Some sort of stomach bug," I said.

"Um-hmmm." She smiled as she clicked the keys on the register.

"No, seriously! Plus, it's such a good sale," I said wryly.

"Mmmm, so I've heard."

Pat and Dave paid for the last eight-pack using similar conversational diversion tactics. My guess is the clerk wasn't buying it. At the same time, she wasn't denying sales either. I began to think we might actually be able to pull this off after all. When we reached the parking lot, we laughed and high-fived each other in celebration of our paper product acquisitions. For us, the purchase itself was a brazen act of teenage rebellion. Not quite along the lines of launching Molotov cocktails at a political protest or skipping school, but for a bunch of straights, this was pretty much living on the edge.

We jumped in Dave's car and piled all the toilet paper in the back seat. One thing is for sure, if we were stopped by a cop, we would have a lot of explaining to do. Short of proving one of us owned stock in Scott Tissue, we would probably be hauled down to the station and our parents called. The cheap thrill of this teenage lawlessness was energizing. Stupid for sure, but energizing too.

Dave drove the half-mile to Stan's house. We were fortunate to find his house was on the end of the block and it was not a terribly well-lighted street. Dave pulled over across the street from the house. Luckily the drapes were drawn in the living room, which opened up to a couple of large trees in the front yard. Both of them would challenge our young arms for sure.

Dave shut the car off and we sat there in the dark for a minute plotting our attack. "Pat, you and Jim take the side yard and Pete, Dan, and I will focus on the front," Dave whispered.

"All right, sounds good. And we'll meet back here in ten minutes. Any more than that is a risk," I said.

We quietly opened the Chevy station wagon doors and slunk over to the house with the eight-packs under our arms. I grabbed my first roll and got it started with a nice three-foot tail. Then I reared back and whaled it skyward at the large tree before me. It sailed like a paper firework, the tail growing longer with each foot of altitude gained. It crested over a large branch and unreeled to the ground. I ran to where it fell, picked it up, tore the paper, and heaved it again. With each throw, it trailed off an insane rainbow of paper as it arced over a tree limb. After only two or three throws the roll was empty. I grabbed another roll, discarding the empty one like a shell casing on the scene of a toilet paper shooting.

I looked over at my buddies. They were running from throw to throw just like me. We were like deranged Christo protégés working on a piece of living art; art that would exist only for a few days, less if it rained. We were consumed with our work and intent on finishing quickly and undetected. The tree papering went on at a breakneck pace for about seven minutes. When we were done, we ran back to the car and clambered in. Dave started the Chevy and rolled off down the street with his lights off so as not to draw attention to us. We looked out the window at our handiwork and laughed uncontrollably. The house looked like something out of Narnia or Alice in Wonderland. We couldn't stop laughing as we drove away. Halfway down the block we looked back to see Stan come storming out of the house. He ran around the house looking to find the perpetrators, just a hair too late.

"Twenty-four rolls!" Dan shouted.

"Stan-the-man looks pretty pissed!" Pete said.

"Twenty-four rolls!" Dave echoed.

It was pretty amazing all things considered. The purchase and execution couldn't have been better scripted. For a bunch of rule-following, Catholic military students, this seemed like a bank heist to us.

The next day at school, Dave slipped a note into Stan Turner's locker that read:

"TP courtesy of the Irish Mafia."

Dave McNeal was always proud of his Irish heritage, so took it upon himself to brand our group. Stan mentioned the note and the toilet papering to a couple of us at lunchtime, but he never did figure out who had done the dirty deed. It pays to have a good poker face.

Now, as wrong as these sorts of hijinks seem to me today, I cannot go back and undo my wrongdoing. I know if I caught some kids doing it to my house I would likely blow a gasket and chase them on foot for a couple of blocks before my heart or legs gave out. It was wrong what we did, but I also think it was part of the whole teen experience. We were stretching the boundaries of responsibility and lawlessness in the pursuit of fun. In our juvenile pursuits, we were becoming young adults and along the way we were building bonds of friendship. Besides, I'm sure there are more teenagers who have done things they wouldn't want their mother to find out about, than those who have not. Teen energy expended doing sometimes stupid things. It's called growing up.

At the same time, I look back on this memory with great fondness. These guys were my best friends. We were all good kids, most days. Academically we were A and B students. Most of us even achieved the student rank of officer at the military school, a position of honor in the JROTC program. Furthermore, we are all Christians, even today. What we learned during those years in the Catholic school system formed our faith and none of us has drifted from the core values of faith, forgiveness (thank God), and redemption. And, while I do feel I owe Stan a much belated apology, I also know my friends and I will sit in our rocking chairs one day with grins on our faces thinking about that night after the football game.

Chapter 16 - City

IT NEVER REALLY OCCURRED TO ME until well into adulthood how lucky I was to grow up in a city like St. Paul. The city's population at the time was around 300,000, which is small enough to be neighborly, even quaint at times, but large enough to have vibrant ethnic diversity and a rich cultural base. People from Minneapolis, its big sister across the river, even sometimes referred to it as St. Small. The '70s were a simpler time and, I would argue, a safer one when kids were left on their own. I'd like to think we were like any other big family of the day, where kids were given a fair amount of leeway to wander throughout the city. But maybe our situation was different, having a mother who worked full time. I don't know. In any case, we traveled by bike and bus and, in our teen years, attempted to look cool cruising around in Mom's Plymouth Volaré. In actuality, we probably looked cooler on our bikes. No, make that definitely cooler on the bikes.

My brothers and I always made it a point to take a few major bike trips every summer. We gathered up a friend or two and set out for distant attractions and natural wonders in our city. Destinations like Como Zoo, the Mississippi River, Minnehaha Falls, or Crosby Park. These were the "faraway places" of my youth that were really only an hour's ride away, but which held the promise of fun, adventure, and exploration. My sisters were never part of these trips. The risk of being seen hanging out with your baby brothers was to be avoided at all cost. My sisters' days of summer were largely spent sleeping in, reading, and hanging out with their girlfriends. Ultimately, they were in charge of watching us as well, so these trips gave them time alone at the house. Three fewer boys around turns *any* summer home into a destination vacation for a teenage girl, so away we went.

Trips like these required entirely too much planning and a generous supply of travel and adventure equipment. We drank Kool-Aid by the tanker truck full and were quick to take advantage of the many free offers on the back sides of the foil Kool-Aid packets. These offers peddled summer vacation gear for ten empty packets, plus a couple dollars to cover shipping. This was gear every adventurous kid needed, like their smiling Kool-Aid pitcher-guy backpack. Made from cloth with a fold-over snap flap, the pack held enough sandwiches, cookies, and chips to nicely fuel the day's efforts. It also accommodated other essentials like fishing bait, a pocket knife, and bike lock.

The backpack was not complete without its accompanying red Kool-Aid canteen. A product of the same special offer series, this item was indispensable. On the day of the trip, one of us mixed up a batch of grape Kool-Aid, filled the canteen, and we were set for a day of guzzling sugar water complete with purple mustaches and permanent stains on our T-shirts. It was the soda pop of our day, kind of a kid's moonshine, handcrafted to the proper sweetness. The stuff was practically on tap at our house continually for ten years. When we weren't drinking it, we were peddling the sweet elixir on the front sidewalk. At fifteen cents a cup, we'd boast to Mom about how we'd made two dollars in a single day selling it. She'd remind us we'd used three dollars' worth of sugar in the process. So much for free enterprise.

Once our equipment was packed, we did a quick inspection of our bikes and made sure they were set to go. We tied our fishing rods under the horizontal frames of the bikes. My tackle box was confined under the rat-trap luggage rack of my three-speed. Others carried tackle boxes in their hands while steering. We took measures to see they were doubly secured with a twist-tie through the latch to avoid having them pop open at an inopportune time while crossing an intersection or jumping a curb. The last thing you wanted was to be picking up Daredevils and bobbers in the middle of the street. En route, our furious pedaling caused the boxes to swing wildly back and forth; a perilous balancing act at any speed.

When all the bicycles were loaded and equipment secured, we rallied our two-wheeled convoy and started out. One of our favorite destinations was Hidden Falls Park on the Mississippi River. The river was about a three-mile ride down Summit Avenue with its stately elms and historic mansions. Summit was a relatively safe street to travel on. It was wide, held a steady thirty-mile-per-hour speed limit for its entire length, and didn't traverse any sketchy neighborhoods. It ended at River Road, another similarly safe stretch that wound along the river bluffs past more large, beautiful homes.

Paul and Rob had Schwinn Stingrays and were kind enough to let me slum around on my big Huffy three-speed. It made for easier pedaling than my brothers, but surely lacked the cool factor of their Stingrays. With a big, gaudy headlight, a rat trap luggage rack, and an odometer that clicked away the miles, my bike was as geeky as they came. It was the bicycle equivalent to an Oldsmobile Ninety-Eight. Big and roomy but about as nimble as a houseboat. It lived up to the splendor of its dirt brown paint job.

We started off down the road toward our destination in single file as close to the curb as possible, weaving out into the traffic lane only when coming upon a parked car. I imagine we were every driver's nightmare, but because we rode in a group, we were at least highly visible. During any given trip, one or another of us fell behind by a half block or so, but typically caught up when the rest of us were stopped by a traffic light.

When we reached the end of Summit Avenue, we took a break at the Civil War monument, a tall concrete tribute to the fallen soldiers. The banks beneath the monument were also a well-known high school kegger spot. "Party tonight at the monument," was an often heard phrase at high schools around the area. The St. Paul police were clued into it as well and kept life interesting for the river revelers of the day. As a bunch of kids on a bike trip, we were quite content to take pulls of grape Kool-Aid from the canteen to cool down.

We took a break at the monument to do a little exploring. We locked our bikes, found a trail through the trees and underbrush of the steep river bank, and walked, slid, and sometimes tumbled down it. Shadow Falls was a small waterfall that ran through the ravine when the water was high enough and we hiked down to it and sniffed around. We never knew what we were looking for, just a bunch of boys checking out the big wide world.

After an hour of exploring around the monument bluffs, we boarded our bikes and continued down River Road, a beautiful winding road with occasional breathtaking overlooks of the big river. We rode past the Ford Truck plant on Ford Parkway, and continued on another two miles to Hidden Falls Park. The road down to the park was steep and twisty, great fun on a bike. On the way down, we stopped at the sandstone caves carved into the side of the river bank. Some of these were naturally formed and others were helped along by human hands. They were simply too irresistible for us to pass up. Within the confines of the asphalt and concrete jungle known as the city, they were a breath of fresh air to us grade school kids on a great adventure.

We nimbly climbed the bank to get to the limestone shelf ledge where the caves were. The walls of the small crawl spaces were covered with graffiti carved into the sandstone. There was everything; expressions of true love, four-letter proclamations, and usually a crude sketch or two of male or female genitalia. Once inside, we tried to add our own initials to the mix, usually losing interest along the way, leaving some unfinished declaration reading "Jim is co." We slithered into and out of the small shallow caves and overhangs, looking for anything interesting inside or around them. We never found much more than cigarette butts and beer cans. Evidently, the early cave dwellers enjoyed Miller High Life and Marlboros as much as modern man. Despite the litter, it was great to imagine we were the first people to have found these places.

When we tired of the caves, we slid down the embankment, hopped back on our bikes, and rode them to the bottom of the hilly drive, where the park was. The main picnic area was ringed by a parking lot, a boat launch, and a spattering of creosote-crusted grills, each with an accompanying picnic table. We dumped our bikes on the shore area next to the boat landing and skipped rocks at the river's edge. We took turns seeing if one of us could throw a rock all the way across the river. Our results were consistently disappointing. Most of them plunked in at about the halfway point.

On a flat rock near the water's edge, we opened a can of whole kernel corn to use as bait. We baited our hooks by meticulously threading as many kernels as would fit. Next, we added sinkers to the line about a foot above the hook. We used the largest ones we could find in our tackle boxes. With the river's strong current, it was important to know the bait was sinking to the bottom where carp liked to feed. The large sinkers also gave some weight to the line, making it easier to cast. Some of us used four or five to give it enough heft to cast it out into the deeper water where the fish were.

As we prepared our lines, barges chugged up and downriver. I loved watching the tugboats pushing multiple barges tethered together to make a single, long boat through the muddy brown water. Barges are the cruise liners of the river and they rule it; all craft yielded to them. The best part of these great vessels was the effect they had on the shoreline where we stood. When they were directly in front of you, the water at the shore's edge would begin to wane toward the middle, as the barge essentially pushed it farther down the river. The water level usually dropped several feet. A few seconds after the boat fully passed, the resulting wake backlash hit the shores with thundering force. It turned an otherwise sleepy shoreline into a momentarily raging one.

When the fishing lines were ready, we reared back with our rods and heaved the corn bait as far as we could into the fast-moving current. Each of us eased a little more line out, trying to keep things at a decent depth. Then, we propped our rods up on shore using some large nearby rocks, making sure they were spaced out along the shore so as not to tangle our lines. Before long, we were set up for a winsome carp harvest. Carp are recognized as perhaps the most abhorrent fish in the state; the Rodney Dangerfield of the fish world, they get no respect. So, in truth, what we had assembled was more like a lineup of shame—carp fishing is as low as you can go—but even crummy carp fishing beats not fishing, every time.

After a half hour or so on one occasion, Rob's rod tip bent violently, signaling the wait was over. Rob had wandered off out of boredom, but was keeping one eye on his line nonetheless. He turned around just in time to see it arcing like a drawn bow.

"Holy crap!" Rob said as he ran to tend it. Before he got there, the rod fell over and was dragged toward the water. He picked it up from the sandy shore and began to reel in his catch.

"Hey, look, Rob's got one," I told no one, and everyone.

Rob was rife with all the excitement of a kid with a big fish on the line. The fish instinctively swam downriver creating exciting, arduous runs for Rob. Carp can grow quite large and when combined with the current of the river can put up tremendous fights. All us boys stopped what we were doing and watched the battle. Rob enjoyed being in the spotlight and fought the fish with drama and a smile on his face. It put up a spectacular fight, slowed down with a few more short runs and eventually tired and was pulled into shore. To say it was a beautiful fish would be a mixed message. With its droopy, Jagger-esque lips and dingy brown scales, it was as ugly as a mud fence, and weighed in at the three to four pound range.

After fishing, we staked out one of the nearby picnic tables and dug into our backpacks for peanut butter and jelly sandwiches and Oreo cookies and we washed it all down with Kool-Aid. After lunch, we did more exploring, fished a little more, and looked for fossils and agates at the river's shore. If we were really bored we'd find a dead fish to poke with a stick because, well, why not? As the afternoon waned, we packed up our gear and headed home. We pedaled furiously in an effort to get a running start up the park's winding hill. By the halfway point, most of us were walking our bikes, giving in to the pull of gravity and fatigue. Once at the top, the rest of the ride home was a focused affair. Most of us were tired from a long day of riding and exploration. We pedaled with abandon, cutting corners where we could, violating traffic laws as judgment led, all in the name of shaving some time off our ride. When traffic got tight, or a situation looked dangerous, we jumped the curb onto the safety of the sidewalk.

As benign as these trips seem now, I realize they were an instrumental part of growing up. My brothers and I were striking out on our own, stretching our stakes, and nourishing our wanderlust. It was a way of establishing our independence in a relatively safe way. We were grade school gypsies in search of a thrill on a long summer's day. Our bicycles took us places too distant for our feet. They transported us to places of beauty, wildness, and wonder, with our legs providing the push and our imaginations steering the way.

***

THE TWIN CITIES ALWAYS supported a respectable showing of professional sports teams. The Vikings were Mom's and Jack's team, a perennial playoff contender from year to year with Fran Tarkenton and the Purple People Eaters. For hockey we had the Minnesota North Stars, who struggled during my boyhood years, but had some good players for sure. And then there were the Minnesota Twins, who had some good years in the mid to late '60s, but were mostly a middle to bottom of the pack team in the '70s. None of us had much time for the Twins, with the exception of my grandmother, Dagny. She was a Twins nut.

Dag, as we called her for short, was the only grandmother I ever knew. My maternal grandma, Helen, passed away when I was quite young, which added to Mom's list of tragic losses during the early to mid-'60s. Anyways, Dagny was a warmhearted person who was known to be, well, sorta flighty, one might say. At the same time, she was so sweet and kindhearted you could always forgive her flightiness. She had a laugh exactly like Barney Rubble of *The Flintstones*, but carried herself with elegance and class. One thing was certain, though, she was Minnesota's worst driver. Everyone in my family has a story or two about Dag's driving and we were all in agreement that much of her problem stemmed from having a car that was too big for her. She was the classic case of the apparent driverless "hands on the steering wheel" you saw when following the Chrysler New Yorkers or Lincoln Town Cars of the world. The sheer size of the vehicle took her just a little too far away from the real world. Too much glass and steel around some people is not a good thing. Insulated from reality and the havoc she created in the traffic lanes around her made for some hairy rides as a kid.

I'll never forget the ride out to Met Stadium to take in a Twins game one year. Because she was a season ticket holder, she always made a point to take Rob, Paul, and me to a game every season. We always enjoyed these outings, in part because she had access to the Stadium Club, a restaurant and bar that were exclusive to members only. It made us feel a little above the rest of the minions that entered through the turnstiles. But as much as we looked forward to these outings, it always meant a white knuckle ride in the old New Yorker. This trip would be no different.

Being the oldest of the three of us boys, I took the front seat while Rob and Paul piled in the back. Looking back, this was probably not a great decision on my part, but someone had to do it or we risked Dag wondering why everyone was in the back seat. We cruised down Lexington Parkway as Dagny made small talk and unknowingly drifted over the lane stripes like a rudderless boat adrift on a winding river. When she floated toward the curb or a parked car on the passenger side of the road I found myself leaning toward the center of the car, like a motorcycle passenger, as if to will the car back toward the center of the lane. I couldn't see Rob and Paul in the back seat but I suspect they were doing some leaning of their own. It had all the excitement of a carnival ride and Dag was our resident carny.

We took a right turn onto West Seventh Street, a busy, four-lane arterial road dotted with stoplights and traversing from downtown St. Paul all the way to the Mississippi River. As we approached a stoplight, Dagny started to brake, but from my perspective, it seemed to be too late. The light was located on the far side of the intersection and we were almost entirely through it before she stopped. When we finally did, the stoplight stood a few feet away from her right fender. If you wanted to see when the light changed, you'd have to duck your head and look almost directly overhead to see what color it was. We were essentially under the light.

Now, at that age, I was too young to drive, but I knew this was not how it was supposed to work. From my seat, it was brutally apparent we were in the middle of the intersection. By the grace of God, there were no cars trying to enter it from my right. As we sat there awkwardly, Dag appeared oblivious to her driving blunder and just sat there gripping the wheel at the ten and two positions. Knowing lights could take two to three minutes to change, I felt compelled to say something before the embarrassment became life threatening.

"Um, I think we should have stopped back there by the crosswalk, Dag," I said, hoping she wouldn't think of me as a know-it-all.

"What?"

"The light. I don't think we're supposed to stop here. I think we're supposed to be back there," I said, pointing toward the back window.

"Uh-oh. Oh my. Oopsie," Dag replied. She swiveled her head around to make sure I was indeed right, and then stepped on the gas, effectively finishing off the running of the red light. Then, she giggled her Barney Rubble laugh and shrugged like it was no big deal. Her laughter served to lighten the mood and made a tense moment bearable. Rob, Paul, and I laughed nervously along with her as we whisked along down the road to the old ball game.

***

MINNESOTA HOSTS ONE OF THE BIGGEST and best state fairs in the nation. It is an eleven-day affair that takes place on the state fairgrounds in Saint Paul, a little less than four miles or a forty-five-minute bus ride from our house. We loved to hang out at the fair if for nothing else than to break up the monotony of late summer and gorge ourselves on corn dogs, snow cones, and cotton candy. I went with my brother Tom and a friend one late afternoon in '73. Mom allowed him to go with a friend, if he took his little brother. So, dressed in jeans and short sleeves, we walked to Grand Avenue and boarded the 3A bus. I was eleven and Tom and his friend were seventeen.

Tom pulled the buzzer at the Snelling Avenue stop and when the bus hissed to a stop we pushed through the doors and exited to the busy street corner. After a short wait at the stop, the 84 came into view and we rose to make ourselves known. The bus pulled up, its doors slapped open, and we stepped on. Handing the driver our wrinkled transfers, he checked them for legitimacy and we headed to the first open seats we could find. It was crowded with other fairgoers, so we were forced to separate and sit next to strangers. By the time we approached the stop at Como Avenue at the southern entrance to the fair, it was standing room only. People gripped the overhead handrails and held on in fear of falling during one of the many jerks and starts. As the bus slowly emptied, the anticipation grew in my chest. I loved the state fair, and today the plan was to cover it from end to end with my big brother and his friend.

We started at the all-the-milk-you-can-drink-for-a-dime stand. Minnesota was a big dairy state, so this was a popular destination. It was especially so to those of us on a limited budget. For a dime, we were given an approved paper cup filled with Minnesota's finest nectar. When we finished, we got back in line and waited it out for another cup. After about the fourth trip the exercise began to reveal itself as just a tad bit of the insanity that it was. If we wouldn't drink four straight cups of milk at home, what would possess us to do it outdoors at the fair? I think it has something to do with freeloading cheapskates, but I'm not sure.

"Let's go to the penny arcade," Tom said.

"Sounds good!"

Jim Landwehr

As we walked down the streets with the lightly sweating throngs of humanity it was difficult to take it all in. Pungent-smelling fried onions at the foot-long hotdog stand co-mingled with the sweet aromatic goodness of cinnamon-and-sugar-coated Tom Thumb donuts. People of all shapes and sizes ambled by pushing strollers, drinking beer, or holding food on a stick. Many of them carried the extra weight they gained at last year's fair and never lost. Cranky children overdue for a good nap grasped balloons given away at the television booth. Adults and children alike donned cheap paper visors acquired at the grandstand exhibition hall. The whole spectacle was a carnival of crazy, a festival of foodliness, and nothing short of intoxicating for a kid my age.

As we passed stand after stand of merchandisers and hawkers promising personal gain—three tries for a dollar—carnies and vendors vied for our money and attention. "No, no thanks," we said politely. We knew much of our money was destined for a three-minute tryst with an electronic pinball whore. After a short walk, we arrived at the penny arcade where the clicking, ringing, and dinging was deafening. Lights flashed, sirens shrilled, and shots rang out in a sort of electronic street riot. Having never been exposed to this level of game intensity, I was awestruck. Pairs of teens were everywhere watching each other do battle against the pinball bumpers, the virtual racetrack and the clawed crane's false promise of a stuffed animal. I had a few dollars to spend, and the choice of which machine to flush it into was almost too much. The allure of a three-minute entertainment shot to the cerebral cortex a quarter at a time took over my sense of self control.

I strolled over to the row of pinball machines. Some were decked out with seductive-looking women scantily dressed, wooing young eyes like twenty-five-cent hookers. Others featured gambling themes with names like Hi Lo Ace and Monte Carlo. I plugged a random machine and started banging flippers like my life depended on it. Within a couple of minutes, I drained all three balls and stood there looking at my paltry score and feeling a strange mix of elation and disappointment. It didn't take an eleven-year-old to spot the fact that the games appeared slanted heavily in favor of the house there.

I sauntered away from the machine like a penny arcade crackhead in search of my next cheap fix. Determined to make my dollars stretch, I went over and watched a couple of the black and white nickel movies, which ranged in style from Chaplinesque short films to burlesque shows featuring curvy dancers from the '30s dancing about in flouncy bloomers and boas. The pictures were without sound, so were either badly captioned or completely silent. These thirty-second movies were usually worth about what you paid for them. It was clear if you wanted good entertainment, it was going to cost you a quarter.

After another half an hour of the three of us simultaneously plugging the multitude of electronic bandits, we moved on to better things. This teenage Las Vegas disguised as the Penny Arcade sucked not only from my pockets but nipped at the innocence of my pre-teen soul, as well. The whole experience left me flat. It was like sex without love, a momentary pleasure that felt good on the outside, but left a gnawing feeling on the inside, like I'd just been suckered, which in essence, I had. We all had.

From the arcade, we wandered down the avenue in the direction of the Midway. In the distance we heard a truck revving repeatedly, over and over. Rooooooarrr, braaaap! Rooooooarrr, braaaap! We heard the deafening sound from two blocks away. When we arrived at the source of the racket we found a large semi-truck and trailer painted blue and white. Over the loudspeaker a recorded message played over and over an advertisement about Irvy the Whale. It went on about how "Irvy was found off the coast of . . . blah, blah, blah." The hook line that stuck in my head was, "If Irvy the Whale isn't real, we'll give you the truck."

Because everyone needs a semi with a whale in it parked in their driveway.

Tom had seen Irvy in years prior and described it to me as a rip-off. This description, coming after the Penny Arcade bloodletting, served to reinforce my distrust of the entire product line I was being fed at the fair. As the evening wore on we walked the fair from end to end. Other than a marginally successful outing at the mechanical Dragline cranes where Tom managed to successfully snag a couple of Zippo style lighters for a quarter each, we mostly just bled money at one stand or another. And while I realize this is what the fair is all about, namely spending large amounts of money on overpriced gratifications, it served to educate me a little on my street smarts. As I was pulled in the direction of a host of seemingly brain-dead easy carnival games, Tom explained the way in which each was rigged in the house's favor. It was an education in how not to be the sucker. It yanked me out of my trusting innocence and taught me there is no such thing as a free lunch. Heck, even free milk costs a dime. But the fair also taught me sometimes you can find some pretty good life lessons between the corn dog stand and the world's smallest man.

Chapter 17 - Violation

IT IS HARD TO PINPOINT exactly when the idea of downsizing started niggling at my mom. The sheer size of the house for a big family like ours was always a bit of a mixed blessing from a maintenance standpoint. After Tom, the handiest of all of us boys, moved out, Mom no longer had the luxury of calling on his expertise at a moment's notice, which made home upkeep even more difficult. A few years later, Pat and Jane moved out, and bedrooms started to open up, especially once Rob went away to school in Rochester, New York, for nine months of the year. Add to these circumstances the fact that Mom's relationship to Jack was becoming strained, in part because of his drinking, and the case for her increasing unrest with our blue collar mansion was becoming clear. I also think it was a series of events in the early '80s that pretty much sealed the deal.

One day after school I arrived back at the house and was puzzled to find the front door wide open. Mom and Jack were in Denver on vacation and nobody was supposed to be home at the time, so it struck me as odd. I walked into the living room and was taken by surprise at what I found inside. The large desk sat looking accosted near the bay window. Every drawer was pulled open and their contents lay on the floor like office supply confetti. My jaw dropped as I stood there wondering who had left this mess. My heart started to race as I realized the chaos looked different from the usual messes that were part of our daily living. This one had a sinister feel to it—a mess of a different sort. I walked farther into the living room and when I looked over to the television table, I saw the TV was missing! The table sat there naked and purposeless. What the heck? Someone took our television? I quickly realized this was a scene I'd come upon before. Someone had defiled our house and taken our stuff, again! We were burglarized a year earlier when someone broke in and took another TV, an Atari game console, and coin collections belonging to Paul and me. A couple of years before that, it was some of Tom's guns as well as his coin collection. Now we had been hit again. I stood there shocked, overcome with a mixture of anger, rage, and fear.

Without thinking, I ran upstairs to see if it too had been burglarized. I looked in Mom's room and found a similar scenario to the living room. The drawers of her dresser were all pulled open, and a few of them lay on the floor. Mom's clothes were strewn about, creating the look of a college dorm room after a panty raid. Her jewelry boxes were all emptied of their contents. One of her pillow cases was missing, apparently used to hold some of the stolen items. These perpetrators had evidently done this kind of thing before. I also noticed the window in her room was wide open. It led out to a flat roof over the kitchen. Looking back, it's my guess now this was the entry point of the pond scum who did that to our house. Unfortunately, that didn't occur to me at the time.

I checked the other bedrooms and they were ransacked as well. When I went into my room, I saw my brand new stereo equalizer was missing from my rack of stereo components. Not my equalizer! The rest of the components were left unscathed, but I had really grown to love this most recent addition, so it made me fume into a good lather.

I ran back downstairs and called Mom at the number she had left us scrawled on a note on the refrigerator. She hadn't yet arrived in Denver, so I left a message to have her call me. When she finally called an hour later, I answered the phone ecstatic that I could tell someone about what I found.

"Mom, we've been burglarized again!"

"What? Oh my gosh, again? What happened?"

"The house is trashed. They took the TV, your jewelry, my stereo equalizer and who knows what else. There are clothes everywhere. It looks like they were in every room. I don't know how they got in. I'm so mad I want to kill the guy who did this!" I said frantically.

"It's okay, hon. Calm down. Is anyone else home?"

"No, not yet."

"Well listen, I want you to call the police and get out of the house right away."

"Oh, they're long gone. At least I think they are," I replied. It occurred to me I had never thought twice about the possibility of someone still lurking in the shadows somewhere.

"I don't care. I'd feel better if you got out of there and notified the police. I'm on my way home now."

"All right, I will."

I looked up the number for the police and dialed it on the rotary phone in the kitchen. When they answered, I told them we had been burglarized and gave them our address. After a short exchange in which the dispatcher reminded me to get out of the house, she said they would send a squad out as soon as possible. Within a half an hour a squad arrived and a couple of officers came to the door. They took my statement, dusted for prints in a couple of locations, and looked for footprints in the mud on the side of our house. From an insider's perspective, the officers seemed fairly indifferent to the magnitude of our situation. It was almost like this was routine and they did this kind of thing every day or something. Didn't they know that this was *our* house? *My* house? *My* equalizer!

After the cops took down all of our information, they said they would file a report, but that there was little chance of catching the guys, as they didn't have much evidence to go on. It seemed like an ineffectual response to our plight, but what else could we do? The whole experience of having our home entered by strangers, who proceeded to ransack the place and take items that were not theirs, was disturbingly unsettling. The mere thought of them walking around the place was creepy enough, in and of itself. A home is a place of security and safety. To have it violated and defiled in such a strong-armed way left us all a bit jittery. We slept a little less soundly and tended to look at friends and strangers with side-eye and just a hint more suspicion than in the past.

Unfortunately, we didn't learn from the first two burglaries. Despite taking increased precautions, we still fell victim to new points of entry. Deadbolts on the doors, iron bars on the basement windows, and a backyard fence along the alley still did not prevent thieves from entering. This indicated it was probably a repeat offender, someone who knew their way around and into our house — an inside job, if you will. We reasoned it was probably an unseemly friend of a friend. Luckily for Mom, most of the items were covered under homeowners' insurance. Nevertheless, this last incident turned out to be the largest of all of the insurance claims.

These break-ins raised our awareness that one's home is one's castle only when the drawbridge is up and the turrets are guarded. They gave all of us a healthy respect for the vulnerability of possessions and personal spaces. It was a reminder that the safe place we call home can be turned upside down in a matter of a few minutes. Ultimately, they also served as the catalyst that provoked each of us to relocate to the relative safety of the suburbs. This is unfortunate, because we all loved Saint Paul, our neighborhood, and the access it gave us to cultural events, businesses, and friends. But when your faith in a place is shaken, especially on multiple occasions, desperate times call for desperate measures.

Chapter 18 - Sold!

ALL OF US KIDS, WITH THE EXCEPTION of Paul, had moved out of the house by the time the "For Sale" sign went up in the front yard. At the time, Mom was in the midst of divorcing Jack and the house had become a huge burden on her both physically and fiscally. The sign was thrust into our lawn and sat there wooing passersby much like it had wooed Mom more than fifteen years prior. The first time he saw the sign, Rob spoke his mind to Mom.

"I do not like that sign out there!" he said, thrusting his finger toward the front lawn.

Mom, taken by surprise at his reaction, spoke in her defense. "Well, we knew this day would come sometime, my dear. I have to get out from under this house, it's just too much for me. Besides, the memories are what make the house, not the house itself. You'll always have those memories and will take them with you wherever you go," Mom said in her calm, practical manner.

The phrase about the memories following us has always stuck with me. Mom had a good point. The places our lives take us, all of them temporary, are but stops on our journey; dwellings we leave behind in our trajectory toward something better. What happens between the walls of those apartments, homes, and shared living spaces forms our experience and makes us who we are. The house is just the framework or the stage for the dramatic theatrical experience we call life.

When the house finally sold, Mom found a two-bedroom apartment on Montreal Avenue a few miles away. We helped her move out well before her appointed date and, before too long, the house sat vacant awaiting its new occupants. During this period, there rose an occasion where I had a chance to stay overnight in it. At the time, I was living in a Minneapolis suburb and when I found out some friends were going out for a nighttime gathering in St. Paul, I figured I would have a place to stay in Mom's house. When I asked her if I could spend a night on the floor, she said I was more than welcome to. She was happy to have someone kind of checking on the place anyways, so it was a win-win.

After the night out with those friends at some of my old St. Paul haunts, I pulled up to the house and parked in front. I am the world's biggest nostalgic, so as I walked toward the house, past events from the front yard came flooding back to me. The time Rob rode his bike off the porch on a bet, the step baseball games, hanging out on the porch, the Wiffle bat bee killing, posing for graduation pictures and more. I thought about the neighbors, good old Mrs. Delaney on the right, mean old Mr. Hagen and his successors, the Flanagans, on the left.

I keyed open the deadbolt and entered my house for what I knew was the last time. It was a strange combination of familiarity and intrusion. Since I moved out a year earlier, I'd returned a few times for visits, but every time I did, I felt just a bit less at home. As much as I wanted to miss the place, there was part of me that had accepted the reality that this chapter in my life had closed. It was a beautiful chapter, full of joy, sorrow, fun, and growth, but one that had surely run its course, played itself out to completion. I had established my new roots in my first apartment and was enjoying the freedom afforded a young, single renter. My trips back home since I moved out were strictly to see Mom and not because I missed the house. That last night there was different, though. I'd taken the opportunity to stay there with the sole intent to reflect, reminisce, and remember.

The house was devoid of furniture. After living in my own bachelor pad for a few months, I had a better understanding that furnishings, artwork, curtains, and the details are what make a house or an apartment feel more like a home. Without those things, your living quarters become a sterile box. To see my old house bare and empty reinforced the notion this was a passing stage in my life.

I decided to take a walk through the house to see what memories bubbled to the surface, partly because I'm a sappy sentimentalist and partly to mourn this place I once called home. In the living room, memories of everyday routines washed over me. The countless TV programs we watched as kids, including the goofy stuff like Saturday morning cartoons enjoyed while munching down bowls of Quisp and King Vitamin. Or those weeknight shows like *All in the Family, Charlie's Angels*, and *Emergency!* And, of course, all of the sick days spent home from school watching *Casey Jones, Let's Make a Deal*, and *Dark Shadows*. All of these were in the days before cable, when even television had a bedtime and every broadcast day finished with the National Anthem.

I thought of all the people and animals that had passed through the living room. Grandparents, uncles and aunts, cousins and stepsiblings. Even a few nieces and nephews had shared time at "Nanny's house," as it was referred to when my mom became a grandparent. Various adopted or rescued dogs, cats, and birds had called this place home and done their part in marking it, chewing it, or soiling it as such. The faces and personalities of these people and pets seemed as real to me in that empty living room that night as they were over the years we had lived here. These spaces made the faces, one might say.

I wandered into the dining room, which seemed strangely expansive and hollow without the antique dining room table in it. My mind rewound to Thanksgiving, Christmas, and Easter dinners, which were almost exclusively the only meals eaten in that room. The dining room always held the "adult table," while most of us kids were relegated to the kitchen or even living room card table setups. The beautiful chandelier still hung in the middle of the room, giving it a regal elegance despite its cavernous emptiness. One of the more notable missing items was Mom's large circular gold-framed mirror.

She spent every morning in front of it spraying her clouds of Aqua Net, doing her part to shoot tiny holes in the ozone one day at a time. It was her last stop before she left for work, making sure she had everything together from a fashion and cosmetic standpoint. Without the mirror and the antique wooden buffet beneath it, it was just another empty white wall.

I moved into the kitchen. It, too, was sterile and quiet. Missing was the aroma of Mom's pot roast simmering on the stovetop and the cacophony of kids chattering around the avocado green Formica-topped dinner table. I thought of all of the birthdays celebrated there, most of them featuring a 9"x13" yellow Betty Crocker cake-from-a-box frosted with canned chocolate frosting. Mom didn't have much time for baking, but it didn't bother us kids. We never had a problem with *any* cake.

The cheap flower petal plug-in clock that had graced the back wall as long as we lived there no longer hung as a reminder that we would be late for school if we didn't slam down our Froot Loops, grab our books, and run. The walls and ceiling were bare and freshly painted, giving no clue of the bacon grease flash-fire incident I had caused several years earlier. That was a secret the new owner never needed to know about. Some secrets are best kept in the family.

All of the house parties I ever held usually ended up in this kitchen. For some reason, it seemed to attract people as a meeting place. Perhaps it was because that was where the beer was usually set up. Or maybe it was because the stereo was blaring George Thorogood and people needed a refuge. Whatever the case, it always ended up smelling like a frat house the morning after these gatherings, but nothing a bit of Lysol and a sponge mop couldn't fix. As I stood there, the sensible vinyl floor that replaced our dirty harvest-gold carpet a few years prior was spotless, ready for the new owners.

I grabbed my sleeping bag and went upstairs. I threw my bag into my old room and wandered over to what used to be Rob and Paul's room. Thoughts of playing electric football with my friends

Marty and Mitchell came to me as I walked in. Strangely enough, the other prominent memory from this room was Rob's phonograph playing Kenny Rogers' "The Gambler," and Queen's "Another One Bites the Dust" over and over again. With his hearing loss, when Rob found songs which he could feel the beat and learn the words to, he latched on and beat the song to death. I thought it was an odd thing to mark about the room. Why a record player and those particular songs? It's my guess the combination of music and place has an impactful, more lasting effect on a brain than just one or the other alone. I don't know.

I went into the adjacent bedroom. It was my mom's room but I still considered it Pat and Jane's room. They occupied it for the first many years and, for some reason, that's how I'd chosen to remember it. I recalled the 9"x13" cake pan hidden with cigarette butts under Pat's bed and the cheap white vanity that they had for years against the near wall as you entered the room. The furniture piece had pull-out arms decorated with lavender-colored curtains that covered a drawer for storing makeup and girl things. The vanity top was always littered with makeup wands, curling irons, nail polish, and a lighted mirror. It was a feminine zone that was off limits to us boys, for good reason. None of us much entered the estrogen zone of this room for fear of retribution; the cost was much too high.

Next, I moved on to what was my mom's original bedroom. Like Jane and Pat's, it had become Paul's room, but would continue to be Mom's in my mind forever because it was her room before his. I thought of the breakfasts in bed we'd served Mom on Mother's Day. These surprise meals of bacon, eggs, toast, and juice were usually spearheaded by Jane. Mom was always courteous about accepting our gift and eating away, even though it is probably every mother's nightmare—crumbs or spilled juice in the bed. Kind of a weird thing if you think about it. I remember her room as always being the "clean room." The rest of us lived like bohemians and our sleeping quarters were proof. Mom's was always pretty tidy and with a big dresser and queen bed combination, she clearly had the best digs in the house, as she should. Queen Mary.

It was a strangely comforting experience walking through the house one last time. Just being in Mom's room, albeit empty, brought back a sense of place and belonging. At the same time, it was eerily empty and hollow. If it wasn't for these memories burrowed deep in my mind, this would be just another empty box inside a larger box of them.

Tired from my day, I moved onto my old room, got undressed, turned out the light, and climbed into my sleeping bag. As I lay there, the history of the house continued streaming through my consciousness. I thought of the pets and the pranks, the laughter and the tears, the happiness and the sickness. The many hours I spent in my own room building models, studying for high school and college, and blasting my stereo were coming to a close on my final night in it.

My mind raced there in the vacant confines of my former bedroom, and in the flow of thought, what Mom had said surfaced again and I knew she was right. A house is just a container for the actions and beauty and love that comprise the life of a family over time. The family members within it change places and each of them carries an explicitly different experience to their new homes. Sometimes they start families of their own, then build their new surroundings into their own private little kingdoms using the subconscious influence of the very homes they just vacated. Little did I know that in a mere eighteen months, I would take a job in Waukesha, Wisconsin, and leave my home state to start a new life and a successive series of new homes there. And while these new homes were also difficult to leave, there was something especially hard about saying goodbye to my boyhood home. It seems the whole moving process is a joyously sad circle.

Move, live, repeat.

This final walk-through made it clear that even though I was in my house, my home was in my heart and mind. I carried it with me. I realized I was fortunate enough to have spent nearly fifteen years in that house with five extraordinary siblings and a heroic mother who helped shape my experience as well as my character. Our big family filled the house for a time and made it ours. Soon enough, some strange family of people who know nothing of the joy and love and pain that unfolded between these walls would move in and make it their own. I could only hope they would appreciate it as much as I did. Because I knew, as much as I hated the thought of it, in the morning the house would be part of my past forever.

As I lay there alone, crying, I realized I was also restored in part by this place, this building, this structure, and was thankful for the life it had given me. It was nothing special to anyone but our family and, at the time, that was quite enough. I rested quietly in the hope that someday I would have a house of my own that would equal the legacy of this one. Because, in all of its middle class humility, the Portland house was just perfect.

THE END

About the Author

JIM LANDWEHR'S first book, *Dirty Shirt: A Boundary Waters Memoir*, was published by eLectio Publishing in 2014. He also has two published poetry collections, *Written Life* (eLectio Publishing) and an ebook, *Reciting from Memory*. His nonfiction has been published in *Main Street Rag*, *Prairie Rose Publications*, *Boundary Waters Journal*, and others. His poetry has been featured in *Torrid Literature Journal*, *Off the Coast Journal*, *Blue Heron Review*, and many others. He enjoys fishing, kayaking, and camping with his kids in the remote regions of Wisconsin and Minnesota. Jim lives and works in Waukesha, Wisconsin, with his wife, Donna, and their two children, Sarah and Ben. He works as a GIS Analyst for the Waukesha County Department of Parks and Land Use.

CPSIA information can be obtained
at www.ICGtesting.com
Printed in the USA
LVOW11s1924300418
575398LV00004B/1069/P